T0330155

How Business Organizes Collectively

NEW HORIZONS IN ORGANIZATION STUDIES

Books in the New Horizons in Organization Studies series make a significant contribution to the study of organizations and the environment and context in which they operate. As this field has expanded dramatically in recent years, the series will provide an invaluable forum for the publication of high-quality works of scholarship and show the diversity of research on organizations of all sizes around the world. Global and pluralistic in its approach, this series includes some of the best theoretical and analytical work with contributions to fundamental principles, rigorous evaluations of existing concepts and competing theories, stimulating debate and future visions.

Titles in the series include:

Career Dynamics in a Global World
Indian and Western Perspectives
Edited by Premarajan Raman Kadiyil, Anneleen Forrier and Michael B. Arthur

How Standards Rule the World
The Construction of a Global Control Regime
Ingrid Gustafsson

How Business Organizes Collectively
An Inquiry on Trade Associations and Other Meta-Organizations
Hervé Dumez and Sandra Renou

How Business Organizes Collectively

An Inquiry on Trade Associations and Other Meta-Organizations

Hervé Dumez

Professor in Management Studies, Institut Interdisciplinaire de l'Innovation (i3), CRG-École polytechnique, CNRS, IP-Paris, France

Sandra Renou

PhD Student in Management Studies, Institut Interdisciplinaire de l'Innovation (i3),CRG-École polytechnique, CNRS, IP-Paris, France

NEW HORIZONS IN ORGANIZATION STUDIES

Cheltenham, UK • Northampton, MA, USA

Published by
Edward Elgar Publishing Limited
The Lypiatts
15 Lansdown Road
Cheltenham
Glos GL50 2JA
UK

Edward Elgar Publishing, Inc.
William Pratt House
9 Dewey Court
Northampton
Massachusetts 01060
USA

A catalogue record for this book
is available from the British Library

Library of Congress Control Number: 2020937692

This book is available electronically in the **Elgar**online
Business subject collection
DOI 10.4337/9781839106682

ISBN 978 1 83910 667 5 (cased)
ISBN 978 1 83910 668 2 (eBook)

Printed and bound by CPI Group (UK) Ltd, Croydon, CR0 4YY

Contents

Tables

Abbreviations

ADEME	Agence de l'Environnement et de la Maîtrise de l'Énergie (French Public Environment and Energy Management Agency)
ASAE	American Society of Association Executives
CONCAWE	CONservation of Clean Air and Water in Europe
CPE	Contrat de Première Embauche (First Employment Contract)
CRE	Commission de Régulation de l'Énergie (Energy Regulatory Commission)
CSI	Cement Sustainability Initiative
CSR	corporate social responsibility
EEB	Energy Efficiency in Buildings
EITI	Extractive Industry Transparency Initiative
ESAE	European Society of Association Executives
FACE	Fonds national d'Amortissement des Charges d'Électrification (National Fund for the Amortization of Electrification Charges)
FCAD	firms' collective action device
FEE	France Énergie Éolienne (French Wind Energy Association)
GATT	General Agreement on Tariffs and Trade
GBC	Global Business Coalition
GBI	Global Business Initiative
GPPN	Global Public Policy Network
GRI	Global Reporting Initiative
ICC	International Chamber of Commerce
IGO	intergovernmental organization
INTERBEV	Interprofession Bétail et Viande (Livestock and Meat Inter-branch)

METI	Ministry of Economy, Trade and Industry (Japan)
NGO	non-governmental organization
NIMBY	not in my backyard
OECD	Organisation for Economic Co-operation and Development
OFATE	Office Franco-Allemand pour la Transition Énergétique (French-German Office for Energy Transition)
PAC	political action committee
QCA	qualitative comparative analysis
RE	renewable energy
SBCI	Sustainable Building and Construction Initiative
SER	Syndicat des Énergies Renouvelables (Trade Association of Renewable Energies)
SIPROFER	Syndicat des Industriels et Professionnels Français des Énergies Renouvelable (Trade Association of French Renewable Energies Industrialists and Professionals, now known as SER)
UNGC	United Nations Global Compact
VPSHR	Voluntary Principles on Security and Human Rights
WBCSD	World Business Council for Sustainable Development

1. Introduction

This book is an inquiry into how firms organize themselves collectively through trade associations, chambers of commerce, and other types of organizational devices, to carry out joint actions. The topic might seem marginal, yet it is important for our economies and modern societies. In the Middle Ages, guilds united artisans or merchants to protect their common interests and played a political role in cities and even throughout kingdoms. But, after the end of the eighteenth century, the firm began to be seen as an individual entity that operates on the market in competition with its rivals, with little cooperation between them. This situation has been reinforced by antitrust laws (competition policy in Europe) that prohibit certain collective trade practice, or closely supervise them in order to monitor the distribution of economic power and ensure healthy competition. Only in the relatively recent period – for example, for environmental reasons – has collective action taken place between firms (Rajwani, Lawton & Phillips, 2015).

This, situation, however, is highly nuanced. As early as the eighteenth century, when the modern economy took off, trade associations and chambers of commerce emerged. These two organizational forms spread quickly and on a large scale during the nineteenth century. Collective action between firms (Astley & Fombrun, 1983) is thus a surprisingly stable element in time, and consequently probably central to the economy and modern societies – some authors speak of a "corporative-associative order" (Streeck & Schmitter, 1985a, 1985b). Because of antitrust laws, however, this collective action involves only non-market strategies (Baron, 2006, 2016) such as lobbying or influence. And, with the intervention of the state in the economy, especially during the two world wars, the phenomenon has strengthened considerably. The recent period, which saw the proliferation of charters and collective actions in the environmental field is not a real turning point, therefore – trade associations had already drafted charters on various problems at the beginning of the twentieth century and some trade associations were already dealing with waste management at that time (Naylor, 1921). The fact that firms, since they have existed, have always developed non-market forms of collective strategies tends to show that the phenomenon is socially, politically, and economically important.

STATE OF THE ART ON FIRMS' COLLECTIVE ACTION

The phenomenon of firms' collective action is not new and has been well studied. Paradoxically, it remains little known. This derives from the fact that this knowledge is extremely dispersed between disciplines (history, political science, economics, management) and even sometimes within a discipline. Some historians, for example, have specialized in the history of trade associations (Aldrich & Staber, 1988; Aldrich et al., 1994; Galambos, 1966; McCormick, 1996). Others have studied chambers of commerce (Bennett, 1995, 2011; Lacombrade, 2002). But even when they have studied both (e.g., Bennett), they have not attempted to analyze them as belonging to a more general category – that of the devices organizing firms' collective action (Berkowitz & Dumez, 2015). Moreover, historians have often not noted the emergence in the recent period of new forms of organizational devices (Berkowitz, Bucheli & Dumez, 2017).

Political science has focused its attention on interest groups (Berry & Wilcox, 2018). Among them are trade associations representing the interests of firms, but also others not involving firms (consumer associations, patients' associations, environmental protection associations, etc.). The category therefore tends to amalgamate firm-specific interest groups with all other types. On the one hand, it illuminates the phenomenon that interests us by placing it in the context of the political philosophy inherited from the eighteenth century and the birth of the first modern democracies with the French and American Revolutions. It allows us to examine the impact of these groups, positive or negative, on the policies carried out in our democracies. It can be used in a symmetrical way at the economic level – Olson (1982), for example, opened up a field of research concerning the possible impact of interest groups, and in particular those that represent firms, on macroeconomic dynamics. On the other hand, the category "interest group" is too broad to account for the specificity of organizations representing firms.

In recent years, organization theory has produced an interesting concept for thinking about collective action between firms – that of the meta-organization (Ahrne & Brunsson, 2005, 2008; Berkowitz & Dumez, 2016; Gulati, Puranam & Tushman, 2012). A meta-organization is an organization whose members are organizations, not individuals. In this sense, trade associations and chambers of commerce belong to this category. Two features characterize this organizational form: there may be a level of competition between the meta-organization and its members (this can be the case between a firm and a trade association at the level of non-market strategies, such as lobbying, for example); moreover, meta-organizations depend heavily on some of their members (if a very large company decides to leave the trade association that represents the sector, the latter cannot really claim to represent the entire sector any longer and may disappear). The notion of meta-organization is therefore particularly useful as an empirical category and as a concept. Nevertheless, two problems arise. On the one hand, trade associations and chambers of commerce functioned throughout the nineteenth century as clubs of business leaders and individual entrepreneurs rather than organizations whose members were the firms themselves. It was not until the beginning of the twentieth century that trade associations and chambers of commerce became real meta-organizations – their members were no longer just business leaders but the companies themselves and they also acquired administrative staff. So, the notion of meta-organization applies to trade associations and chambers of commerce only from this point on. And, like the "interest group," the notion of meta-organization does not just cover organizations supporting the collective action of firms. Ahrne and Brunsson (2005, 2008) give the examples of the United Nations' Universal Postal Union and the European Union. For them, the states are organizations and, as such, the European Union and the Universal Postal Union are meta-organizations.

Several disciplines (history, political science, economics, organization theory, and management) have thus produced a body of knowledge about organizations of collective action between firms. But, if the knowledge is abundant, it is dispersed (these disciplines do not interact a great deal) and the object to be studied is not clearly delimited. Hence this book, which is based on three ideas. First, it is necessary to build an empirical category that sharpens the contours of the phenomenon. Second, we must provide a synoptic view, an overview, of this phenomenon to account for its diversity and its place in our societies. Finally, it is necessary to provide elements of understanding of the functioning of this particular type of organization – the meta-organization.

THE NOTION OF FIRMS' COLLECTIVE ACTION DEVICE (FCAD)

Throughout this book, we will use the expression firms' collective action device (FCAD). We will focus the analysis on the organizational devices that make collective action possible and efficient. Since the beginning of the modern economy, to organize their collective action firms have used two prototypical forms of devices: the trade association and the chamber of commerce. It is as if companies and their leaders needed two things at once to function: to know what is happening in their industry and to defend the collective interest of this industry (hence the trade association); and to know what is happening in other sectors and act in the collective interest of all industries (hence the chamber of commerce). These two fundamental historical prototypes have been stable organizational forms for more than two centuries, but they represent only a part of the diversity of FCADs.

In the recent period, meta-organizations have emerged, bringing together firms from a single industry (and therefore closer to the prototype of the trade association) but specialized in a particular type of problem – for example, environmental. Trade associations, on the other hand, intend to address all the problems faced by firms in the industry, not just a specific problem (Berkowitz et al., 2017). Next are multistakeholder FCADs, in which firms from various sectors (closer to the prototype of the chamber of commerce) often play a key role, but by interacting with other actors – states, non-governmental organizations (NGOs), universities, research centers, and experts. We are now at the boundary of the notion of FCADs, since collective action is taken both between firms and between firms and other actors, which is the principle of multistakeholderism (Raymond & DeNardis, 2015; Utting, 2002). The notion of FCAD therefore allows us to cover the very diversity of organizational forms that collective action between firms can take, up to the boundary situation of multistakeholderism. The construction of this empirical category is the condition for understanding the phenomenon of collective action between firms. It brings together the two historical prototypes – the trade association and the chamber of commerce – and follows the emergence of more recent organizational forms. Using this category, it becomes possible to give a synoptic view of the phenomenon of collective action between firms.

GIVING AN OVERVIEW OF FIRMS' COLLECTIVE ACTION

This synoptic view, as we can see, deals first with history – it is a question of following FCADs from their origin, of seeing how they turned into real meta-organizations at the beginning of the twentieth century, how the two world wars reinforced their role, and then how new forms emerged in the recent period. This historical approach makes it possible to put into perspective the theses according to which the phenomenon would be new or would take on a new scale. But this synoptic view is not reduced to history alone. It is important to understand what can be said about the impact of FCADs on the political functioning of modern democracies and on the dynamics of contemporary economies.

Many researchers argue that to solve current environmental and climate problems – meta-problems in Cartwright's (1987) sense – requires the collective action of firms and therefore the active involvement of FCADs (Nash, 2002; Prakash & Potoski, 2007). On the one hand, there is nothing really new here, as Naylor's (1921) reading shows. On the other hand, the theorists of modern politics and the American and French Revolutions (Madison and Le

Chapelier, respectively), directly inspired by Rousseau, accurately identified the potential problems posed by organized groups for the functioning of democracies – these groups can lean on governments, members of parliament, and public administrations to orient political decisions in the direction of their interests, to the detriment of other, less organized groups or communities. This is the case with the trade associations, often with significant financial means, with regard to the interests of the much more diffused and unorganized consumers. The French revolutionaries therefore decided to prohibit them and during most of the nineteenth century, trade unions and trade associations were banned in France.

Mancur Olson (1982) was the first economist to question the possible impact of FCADs on the dynamics of the economy. His central idea was that trade associations tend to multiply and become institutionalized over time, that they manage to divert the wealth produced by creating rent-seeking situations. Not only is the allocation of resources suboptimal, but growth tends to slow down. The robust growth of the defeated countries after World War II, that of Germany and Japan, could be explained by the destruction of FCADs at the time of the defeat. The empirical studies that followed, however, challenged the results obtained by Olson. Lynn and McKeown (1988), for example, showed the continuity of Japanese FCADs between the pre-war, war and post-war periods – in many industries they persisted, often with the same leaders, by just changing their name.

The overall impact of FCADs on state policies and economies appears difficult to assess. What the synoptic view of the phenomenon shows is that political action must be analyzed and evaluated at the level of subsystems (face-to-face engagement between a public administration and a trade association). At that level, an FCAD can play an important and decisive role in effectively defending the interests of a particular industry.

WITHIN FCADS: THEIR FUNCTIONING, THEIR DYNAMICS, THEIR WAYS OF ACTING

As underlined, this book attempts to bring together the scattered knowledge on the collective action of firms by focusing on the empirical category of FCADs. We must, however, go further and look more closely at these devices by conducting an analysis of their functioning, their dynamics, and their ways of acting.

From a methodological point of view, the task is not easy. FCADs, as we have seen, are diverse. Addressing this diversity by collecting data is both interesting and frustrating. Spillman (2012) did this for American trade associations. She has studied everything that these organizations produce in terms of information, which allows the processing of a mass of data, but, by making this methodological choice, she did not have access to the internal functioning of the trade associations and their actions (lobbying and negotiations with public authorities, for example). We have chosen instead to study the case of a French trade association, the Syndicat des Énergies Renouvelables (SER) – the Trade Association of Renewable Energies. Of course, one case does not reflect the diversity of FCADs. At the same time, the methodological bet is that from one case, one can learn even limited lessons about all other cases – *et ab uno disce omnes*, as suggested by Virgil. Why was this case chosen? Taking a long perspective, as McCormick (1996) did, allows us to understand the dynamics, and in particular to highlight possible periods of dormancy in the functioning of an FCAD. On the other hand, the risk is not being able to interview the actors and to miss the way in which they live the functioning and the dynamics of the organization. And, taking a short perspective allows us to interview these actors but limits the possibility to study the dynamics of the organization during a sufficiently prolonged period. The SER was created in 1993. Our research took place from 2017 to 2019. So, 25 years elapsed between the creation of the trade association and our study. This duration is short enough to have allowed us to meet the actors who created the organization and all the chairpersons who have succeeded them. It is long enough to have given us the necessary time span to highlight the turning points in the dynamics of this device. It is often argued that a trade association "represents" an industry but, at the time of the creation of the organization the industry hardly exists, and, conversely, one might say that it is the trade association that makes the industry exist as much as the industry gives birth to the trade association. It is from this case study that we have tried to understand the functioning of an FCAD as a meta-organization, its dynamics, and its forms of action.

In terms of functioning, the meta-organizations structuring the collective action of firms are very particular organizations. In some ways, they resemble traditional organizations – they have administrative staff, headed by a secretary general or a director general. On the other hand, the facts that the members are firms, that these members seek to avoid or limit any hierarchy between them, that the membership is voluntary and inexpensive, make these organizations profoundly different from a traditional organization, a firm, or even a university or a hospital. They make their decisions based on long negotiations and consensus building, often being threatened with exit by members or a split with the creation of a new meta-organization. To understand this particular functioning, we have mobilized the concept of heterarchy. Hierarchy presupposes vertical relations between the members of classical organizations, with obedience from the lower echelon to decisions taken by the higher echelon (even if, in reality, things are much more complicated – what Mary Parker Follett had already observed well into the 1920s; see Parker Follett, 2013). On the other hand, heterarchy is based on horizontal relations, with the actors having no power to impose something on others, the veto right often being applied, and decisions being taken following long and hard negotiations on the basis of a final consensus. There is probably no pure heterarchy, and, in practice – as is the case in meta-organizations – heterarchy and hierarchy combine. The difficulty is to understand how. Nevertheless, the notion of heterarchy illuminates the functioning of meta-organizations.

But this functioning is not stable over time. Meta-organizations evolve and their dynamics must be accounted for. To deal with this problem, we analyzed the evolution of the SER over 25 years, relying on the experience of the actors we interviewed and using a cost–benefit model of collective action. Joining a trade association involves direct and indirect costs. The direct cost is essentially that of the contribution. It is typically low relative to the company's turnover (and often small businesses pay proportionally less than larger ones). On the other hand, membership also implies indirect costs: the time spent by firms' managers in board meetings, committees, task forces, and so on. This less visible cost can be high when there are a lot of ongoing negotiations. The benefits created by collective action are individual and collective. Individual benefits are the privileged access of the firm to information that may be important to it, the ability to make its voice heard, the possibility to favor or block a decision. All the firms that are members of the FCAD also garner collective benefits: if collective action improves the reputation of the industry as a whole, each firm benefits indirectly. Similarly, if a negotiation with the public authorities leads to a policy favoring the development of the industry or if it results in blocking a political measure that could have affected it, each firm benefits indirectly. The structure of these direct and indirect costs and of these individual or collective benefits evolves over time. It is the main explanatory factor of the complex dynamics of meta-organizations from their creation to their development, through their possible dormancy.

The study of the functioning of FCADs would not be complete if an analysis of their concrete action was not conducted. FCADs, since their emergence, combine a group of distinct functions, which can change over time. The two main ones are the exchange and production of information and the search for an influence on the political, institutional, and cultural environment that surrounds enterprises in general and industries in particular. The two are linked – no influence without the support of information and knowledge, no "pure" information and knowledge without the intention to influence. At the level of influence and lobbying, it is necessary to distinguish the relational, continuous action of FCADs at the relevant administrative and political levels, and the transactional action in the phases of intense negotiations with public authorities. Our analysis shows that the creation of dissymmetry of information and knowledge between the meta-organization and the public authorities is decisive here. Other actions are also sometimes carried out, such as training, research, or market studies.

ORGANIZATION OF THE BOOK

Part I aims to provide a synoptic view of firms' collective action. Chapter 2 is historical; it presents a synthesis of the work of historians on the phenomenon since the emergence of trade associations and chambers of commerce up to the recent period. Chapter 3 examines the place of FCADs in contemporary democracies and economies, relying in particular on research in political science and economics.

Part II studies the trade associations and other meta-organizations that organize firms' collective action. Chapter 4 analyzes FCADs as organizations of a particular type that combine heterarchy and hierarchy. Chapter 5 examines the dynamics of a device since its birth, with its scaling-up phase, its potential dormancy, and the possible creation of another meta-organization through a split. Chapter 6 is devoted to what FCADs do. It introduces the distinction between core and non-core activities and, based on our case study, analyzes non-market collective strategies. Chapter 7 presents new forms of FCADs, comparing, in particular, two multistakeholder meta-organizations: the United Nations Global Compact (UNGC) and the Office Franco-Allemand pour la Transition Énergétique (OFATE – French-German Office for Energy Transition).

The conclusion returns to the synoptic approach and highlights the main results. This is followed by a methodological appendix that, taking stock of all the methodologies used by the different scientific disciplines to study the phenomenon of collective action between firms, specifies how our research was conducted.

PART I

Firms' collective action: a synoptic view

2.   The emergence and evolution of business meta-organizations

The two main types of collective action devices between firms – chambers of commerce and trade associations – appeared at the same time in the late eighteenth century and developed in parallel in the second half of the nineteenth century. Chambers of commerce focus on issues in international trade and were initially created in ports (Bennett, 2011). The creation of the trade associations, however, was related to the appearance of the trade unions and they were initially associations of employers but would soon deal with international trade issues too. The growth of the two prototypical devices took place in the second half of the nineteenth century. Both kinds of devices would become meta-organizations at the turn of the nineteenth and twentieth centuries and both would begin to offer their members services. From that moment, they acquired the characteristic features that remain today. Spillman (2012, p. 347) is therefore right to speak about the "strength and stability of the institution" over more than a century.

In the second half of the twentieth century, new forms of meta-organizations involving companies appeared. They often specialized in particular problems (environment, human rights, sustainable development). They functioned at the sectoral level but also at the infra-, supra-, or cross-sectoral levels (Selsky & Parker, 2005). They may also have been multistakeholders (companies, non-governmental organizations [NGOs], states). We then see family resemblance in the Wittgenstein sense[1] blur the simple opposition between the two prototypes – chambers of commerce grouping companies from very different sectors and trade associations bringing together companies from the same sector. Bennett (2011) has traced in detail the history of chambers of commerce in England, Ireland, and revolutionary America; this chapter will explore the historical dynamics of firms' collective action devices (FCADs) by focusing instead on the starting point of trade associations before addressing the issue of device families that have emerged over time.

THE EMERGENCE OF TRADE ASSOCIATIONS

The collective organization of economic activities is probably as old as the appearance of cities. Traces of this type of organization were to be found in ancient Rome (Bang, 2008) and in ancient China (Liu, 1988). And the streets of European cities also bear witness to this phenomenon – for example, the Quai des Orfèvres in Paris, the Rua dos Douradores in Lisbon, or the Rue des Bouchers in Brussels.[2] The guilds of the Middle Ages controlled entry into the professions, conditions of training, and quality assurance (Epstein, 1991; Foreville, 1985). They created a virtual monopoly of professions, although competition occurred at the margins of cities, in markets and at fairs that attracted merchants and artisans from outside the city for a limited period of time at regular intervals.

The eighteenth century changed the situation. It was hostile to the collective organization for political and economic reasons. The focus was on competition and individualism. Contracts of employment had to be signed between an individual, the entrepreneur, and another individual, the worker, without any other party – neither the state nor a collective of workers nor a collective of entrepreneurs – intervening. From the end of the eighteenth century to the beginning of the nineteenth, the corporate system inherited from the Middle Ages gradually disappeared. In France, the Comptroller-General of Finances, Turgot, prepared an edict abolishing *"corporations"* and guilds in 1776 but he was dismissed by the king before this edict entered into force. It was finally the French Revolution, and the d'Allarde Law of 2–17 March 1791,[3] that suppressed guilds and masterships and freed any individual to practice a trade through the purchase of a license. Nevertheless, the Le Chapelier Law of 14 June 1791 proscribed worker's organizations and banned strikes, so, in effect, the rising professional class had overthrown the power of the aristocracy but not on behalf of the workers. In the same way, the French chambers of commerce, called Conseils de Commerce, that had appeared at the beginning of the eighteenth century were suppressed by the Revolution, although they would be again authorized by Napoléon Bonaparte.

In other countries, the removal of collective organizations occurred a little later – in Sweden, for example, in 1846 (Magnusson, 1994). It appears, however, that clandestine collective organizations operated locally. There were traces to be found in the UK for cotton masters (1745), colliery owners (1780), and book binders (1786) (Yarmie, 1980). This was also the case for the US (Spillman, 2012). In the early nineteenth century, as the large textile factories developed (Freeman, 2018), competition was fierce and individualist philosophy dominated. The period was therefore unfavorable to collective action. But, nevertheless, collective action arose for two reasons: the first strikes and the first labor laws. The first strikes appeared when competition drove down prices and so profits, and when entrepreneurs, to redress these profits, tried to lower wages and further increase working hours. Since factories were concentrated locally, workers could more easily organize to trigger concerted strikes. Faced with these movements, factory owners set up collective action structures.

Their functioning was modeled on the trade unions: each company contributed to the number of employees and machines and, in the event of a strike, the union compensated the company for its losses. This was an insurance system. Informal rules were also set – for example, for maximum wages. Generally, it was agreed not to recognize the trade unions and not to bargain collectively. Blacklists of activist workers were exchanged. These structures were local and transitory: as soon as the strike ended, they disappeared. These were exchange and coordination clubs, not formal organizations.

But, several factors created the conditions for the emergence of permanent collective structures, which after a time took the form of organizations. As noted by Naylor (1917, p. 8): "temporary cooperation leads to permanent organizations." On the one hand, competition led to a certain concentration of production in a number of sectors, with a few large firms providing a substantial share of production. Collective action, which was difficult in a sector with multiple and dispersed firms, became easier. On the other hand, while trade unions were generally banned in most countries,[4] some categories of workers set up permanent structures. This was the case in the UK in 1851 for the Amalgamated Society of Engineers. In response, the Manchester Association of Employers of Operative Engineers was created. It quickly brought together 34 firms representing more than 10 000 workers (Yarmie, 1980).

We are faced with a paradox: was it to defend the *individual* freedom of contracting that employers created, often reluctantly, *collective* organizations? They continued to think of them as temporary, hoping that they could return to the freedom to contract between individuals, but another factor intervened in favor of permanent collective action. From their creation, factories were open to visitors (Freeman, 2018). Dickens, Southey, and Engels visited the first big production units and were shocked by the presence of children and the terrible working conditions (e.g., noise, smell of whale oil burned for lighting, duration of working hours). In 1802, the British Parliament passed the first Factory Act, which limited the workday of apprentices under the age of 21 to 12 hours, although with little means to enforce it. Thereafter, seven other acts on working conditions were successively passed (1833, 1844, 1847, 1850, 1867, 1874, and 1891) and even if this intrusion was timid, a turning point had taken place – the state intervened more directly in the economy. In response, companies organized collectively (McIvor, 1996). It was all about defending a sector against legislation. Sometimes, however, the action was more on the offensive. The Railway Companies Association, founded in 1858, succeeded, for example, in obtaining from the British government the opening of new lines for its members.

In the second half of the nineteenth century, there was another turning point. Gradually, the collective structures became national where they were hitherto local, and permanent where they were hitherto temporary. A new step was taken when the British Mining Association, created in 1854, engaged a solicitor in the early 1870s to follow all legislation that could affect the mines, "as a secretary and a parliamentary watchman" (Yarmie, 1980, p. 226). The trade association then took on its recognized form – it is in permanent discussion with the state and it has staff, albeit minimal. Galambos (1966), who studied the American trade associations in the cotton textile industry, believed that the model of the "dinner-club association", which had no regular staff members and was not a true organization (drawing inspiration from Abbott, 1995, a proto-organization), transformed into a "service" association. It had permanent staff and could therefore offer services to its members. It had become a real organization.

This evolution was reflected in different countries. Japan, for example, was modernizing in the Meiji era, beginning in 1868. In 1876, its banks created their first trade association. In industry, the Japan Paper Manufacturing Federation was set up in 1880. It was then a question of fighting against imports: the federation set the prices, organized exchanges of information on techniques, and prohibited the hiring of competitors' workers. In 1882, the Japan Cotton Spinners' Association was formed, followed by associations for all industrial sectors (Lynn & McKeown, 1988). We can therefore say that at the beginning of the twentieth century the collective action of firms took the form of meta-organizations with three characteristics: they constituted a decided order (as evidenced by their date of official creation); their members were other organizations; and they had permanent staff, albeit minimal, as evidenced by the situation prevailing in the US at that time, which was analyzed for the first time by Naylor (1921).

THE SITUATION IN THE UNITED STATES IN THE 1920S

At the beginning of the twentieth century in the US, trade associations were set up in the politico-economic landscape as meta-organizations. They even played an important part during World War I (their number doubled between 1914 and 1919; Aldrich et al., 1994). The federal state began to control war production by creating the War Industries Board, which relied directly on organizations representing each sector of the economy:

> Because of the legal difficulties caused by having business people serve in an organization that had a voice in the allocation of government contracts, the administration turned to trade association officials as their connections to the private sector. (Lynn & McKeown, 1988, p. 100)

In the US, Emmett Hay Naylor (1917, 1921) studied these organizations. Naylor had studied law at Harvard and was secretary-treasurer of the Writing Manufacturers' Association. According to him, three features characterized these organizations: they were national; they were prohibited from certain practices condemned by the antitrust laws (the Sherman Act was passed in 1890, but several states had voted for provisions protecting competition before this date); and they were real organizations with staff.

Birth and Development of Business Meta-organizations

The story of the emergence of US organizations is similar to what happened in the UK. Employers' associations emerged at the local level in response to labor organizations (Hilbert, 1912; Willoughby, 1905). The first American trade associations tried to set prices and organize market distribution at the local level.[5] It might have been easier at the time to agree on prices at the local level than at the national level, since the US was not an integrated market at the time. When antitrust laws came into force, however, these trade associations were often the subject of the first trials (Sklar, 1990) and many of them were taken to court for conspiracy to restrain competition – see, for example, *Eastern States Retail Lumber Ass'n* v. *United States*, 234 U.S. 600 (1914) (U.S. Supreme Court, 2014). Antitrust jurisprudence developed at the beginning of the twentieth century, which remains largely in force today:

- Prohibition of any discussion of individual members' prices, costs, or factors that might affect prices or costs, sales, inventory, or production data; prohibitions against discussion of allocation of customers or markets or of refusals to serve
- Explicit requirement for formal agenda for every association meeting and for written minutes of every meeting. Prohibitions against off-the-record sessions, secret meetings, or discussion of association business at social gatherings
- Requirement that association staff member be present for every meeting of an association committee
- Requirement that counsel approve the minutes of every meeting so that any association actions that might have anticompetitive effects can be halted
- Discussion of certain areas – eligibility for membership; certain codes and standards; statistical programs; association of cooperative research programs – only in the presence of counsel. (Lynn & McKeown, 1988, pp. 48–9)

From then on, cooperation between firms could therefore be in certain areas to the exclusion of others. Prohibited practices were easier to implement at the local level than at the level of the US as a whole (the case cited above involved, for example, the eastern states of the US). The fact that trade associations became national facilitated their specialization around more economically neutral practices. Two factors led to the change of scale: on the one hand, the workers' organizations themselves became national and, on the other hand, as in the UK, the federal state began to intervene in the economy. Naylor discusses two factors for this change: strikes and tariffs. The chronology of the creation of the first US trade associations is quite clear, as follows, and it overlaps with that of their British counterparts:

1862: the United States Brewers' Association;
1872: the Carriage Builders' National Association;
1878: the American Paper and Pulp Association;
1883: the Laundrymen's National Association of America;
1886: the National Association of Brass Manufacturers;
1894: the National Wholesale Lumber Dealers Association;
1896: the National Association of Retail Grocers;
1908: the American Iron and Steel Institute.

In 1920, Naylor estimated their number (he had tried to conduct a comprehensive census but had a challenging time doing it) to 1000 for the entire US. Their development had been accelerated, as we have seen, by World War I. This development was thus advanced enough that a definition of this kind of organization could be given: "A trade association is an organization for the mutual benefits of individuals who are engaged in the same kind of business" (Naylor, 1921, p. 3). The phrase "same kind of business" is intentionally vague. Indeed, there were trade associations that included manufacturers, wholesalers, and retailers dealing with the same product at different stages. The evolution of trade associations also followed the dynamics of the sectors:

> The American Paper and Pulp Association represents the entire industry. One of its members is the Tissue Paper Manufacturers Association, representing only tissue-paper. Some of these manufacturers who make or convert toilet-paper are members also of a Toilet Paper Converters Association. (Naylor, 1921, p. 43)

There were also geographical subdivisions – for example, for the paper sector, the New England Paper Merchants' Association, the Northwestern Paper Merchants' Association and the Pacific Coast Paper Trade Association. Organizational devices were therefore adapted to the geographical diversity and diversity of production and distribution in each sector. The trade associations were enshrined in each other:

> Particularly when an association represents an industry with many ramifications and independent interests it is generally found desirable for each set of interests to be drawn together into small trade associations, and for the small trade associations to be members of a large co-ordinating national association. (Naylor, 1921, p. 42)

In other words, a trade association often represented several sectors, and a sector was often represented by several trade associations.

Functions of the Meta-organizations

These meta-organizations had two main functions: to liaise with the public authorities, including the federal state, and to produce information (public and private). The link with the state was mostly defensive. It was necessary to avoid the passing of "inimical legislation" (Naylor, 1921, p. 146). At that time, while American industry was still exporting very little, it was necessary to dissuade the state from adopting customs tariffs that could favor foreign competitors. Many American trade associations had set up special committees on tariffs. It was also necessary to try to block the development of trade unions. In the same way, almost all trade associations had a standing committee on labor issues. Members of meta-organizations saw defensive action as easier than lobbying or offensive action. Sector unity was relatively easy to build against a government measure; it was more difficult to obtain when it came to asking for a positive measure. According to Naylor, action against the state was mainly through the production of information on the sector. The ideal was to create a specialized journal on trends in the sector, relatively independent of the association but fed with information by it, which would allow the state to make informed decisions. In parallel, the association had an internal news-letter, reserved for its members, providing them with "intimate information" (Naylor, 1921, p. 128).

In addition to these central functions – influence on government and production and processing of information on the sector – trade associations also had secondary functions. The first was sharing good practices. At the time, exchanges focused on cost accounting. Many American companies did not have an accounting system and did not know how to calculate their costs. It was within the meta-organization that exchanges of practices were organized. Similarly, the business meta-organizations had helped to advance standardization:

> A number of associations, by co-operating with raw material dealers who them-selves have associations, have brought about a standardization of raw materials to facilitate intelligent buying. (Naylor, 1921, p. 114)

Some trade associations had developed research laboratories. This was the case, for example, in the 1920s of the National Association of Master Bakers, which created a research laboratory for making bread, pies and cake with dif-ferent kinds of grains. A 1927 report listed a dozen trade associations that had a laboratory at that time (U.S. Department of Commerce, 1927).

In addition to these functions, trade associations offered their members specialized services. This was particularly the case with regard to insurance advice. Some associations – like the Laundrymen's National Association or the National Retail Hardware Association – had even created their own insurance company. Others had created syndicate buying, as did the Laundrymen's National Association for office machines. Finally, some had created export associations, as in the paper sector with American Paper Exports Inc.

The Internal Organization

A business club becomes a meta-organization when it moves into its own premises and hires a permanent secretary. Already in 1920, this position of secretary had changed its name to general manager or managing director. The function had become professional and a specific labor market had emerged. The role was mainly to manage tensions between members of the association:

> Rumor, gossip, and misinformation generally play a large part in stirring up ill feeling among members which may lead to disastrous results. It must be the secretary's duty to kill the trouble at the start, to forestall the destructive tendencies by quietly and effectively instilling the disposition for harmony in the mind of each member. The secretary should be a constant harbinger of truth. (Naylor, 1921, p. 221)

The office itself could be subdivided into services: statistical, research, credit, and stenographic branches, with someone heading each. Research here meant market research. Most of the time, the association operated within regular standing committees and special committees, the latter generally transient and related to a specific problem (the preparation of a law by Congress). The meta-organization took care to ensure that all members were represented on the various committees.

The Difficulties of Collective Action

In his first analysis of the devices of collective action, Naylor highlighted the operational problems of this type of organization. Naylor, who was himself secretary-treasurer of a trade association, tackled the issue of his difficulties from a humorous angle in a section where he takes up a 1919 article from the Association of Optometrists and Opticians of Quebec, "How to Kill an

Association." Here are some examples of behaviors to adopt to make any collective action impossible:

> Don't come to the meeting; But if you do come, come late;
> If you do attend a meeting, find fault with the work of the officers and other members; Never accept an office, as it is easier to criticize than to do things; Nevertheless, get sore if you are not appointed on a committee; but if you are, do not attend committee meetings;
> Do nothing more than is absolutely necessary; but when other members roll up their sleeves and willingly, unselfishly use their ability to help matters along, howl that the association is run by a clique;
> Hold back your dues as long as possible or don't pay at all;
> When a banquet is given, tell everybody money is being wasted on blow-outs which make a big noise and accomplish nothing; When no banquets are given say the association is dead;
> Don't tell the association how it can help you; but if it doesn't help you, resign;
> If you receive service without joining, don't think of joining;
> If the association doesn't correct abuses in your neighbor's business, howl that nothing is done; If it calls attention to abuses in your own, resign from the association;
> At every opportunity, threaten to resign and then get your friends to resign;
> When you attend a meeting, vote to do something and then go home and do the opposite; Agree to everything said at the meeting and disagree with it outside;
> When asked for information, don't give it; Curse the association for the incompleteness of its information;
> Talk co-operation for the other fellow with you; but never co-operate with him. (Quoted in Naylor, 1921, pp. 93–4)

The verb "to kill" does not refer to the disappearance of the organization (these organizations generally last in time) but to another type of phenomenon we will return to later, which is the dormancy of the organization – formally, the organization continues but in practice is no longer active. This phenomenon remains a problem and it is one of the elements of the modernity of the analysis conducted in 1920.

Modernity of the 1920s

American trade associations of the early twentieth century have features of modernity that are sometimes presented in recent literature on these organizations as novelties. The first is the link with what is now called corporate social responsibility (CSR). Although the expression was not used at the time, the theme was present:

> Every man has some good in him, and most men have qualities that are noble and fine. Business should develop rather than crush these higher qualities, and the trade association is one important means to this end – to help men not only to fill their

pocket-books and to gain material success, but also to grow hearts and souls, and so gain the greater reward of spiritual happiness. (Naylor, 1921, p. v)

In this perspective, already at the time, trade associations tended to share good practices and develop codes of ethics. Such was the case, for example, with United Typothetae of America, the national association of master printers.

The second feature of modernity is the emphasis on the necessary coexistence between competition and cooperation, which Brandenburger and Nalebuff popularized in 1996 under the label of coopetition:

> [The] modern trade association is one result of the business world's realization that unrestricted competition is unnatural and fallacious and that constructive, intelligent competition, together with studied co-operation, is not only desirable but essential to industrial warfare. (Naylor, 1921, p. 28)

Lyn Spillman (2012) is probably right when speaking of solidarity rather than cooperation. The analysis conducted at the beginning of the twentieth century shows that meta-organizations took their place in the American economy at that time. In the period following the publication of Naylor's book, President Herbert Hoover, who belonged to the associationist current of thought, sought a system that had both the advantages of capitalism and freedom of enterprise and collective action. He was a great organizer and was in favor of cooperative institutions, trade associations, and professional societies. He reorganized the Department of Commerce to create a dialogue with trade associations. In 1933, the National Recovery Act sparked a new wave of business association creation and further strengthened their role (the number of staff of the American Iron and Steel Institute, for example, increased from 62 to 80). At this date, trade associations had become what Galambos calls "policy-shaping" organizations:

> This particular form of trade association was distinguished by outstanding leaders, a well-defined and carefully articulated ideology, and formidable cooperative programs. It was a semi-autonomous economic institution with an identity clearly distinguished from its members. In seeking to implement associative values, it impinged forcefully upon individual manufacturers, members, and non-members alike. (Galambos, 1966, p. 292)

In 1938–39, the Temporary National Economic Committee launched a survey of trade associations (Pearce, 1941). Pearce showed that the most common trade association activity, half of which had only one or two staff members, was bargaining with the government: 82 percent of the associations responding reported activity in this area; 45 percent explained that they had contact with congressmen.

AFTER WORLD WAR II

During World War II, economies were run by the states. In Japan, the government and trade associations managed the rationing of raw materials (Lynn & McKeown, 1988). The same phenomenon was observed in France with the Comités d'Organisation set up by the Vichy government, which decided on prices and production (Dumez & Jeunemaître, 1989). In the same way, price controls in the US led to a considerable strengthening of trade associations (Galbraith, 1952). In the ensuing period, their role seemed to diminish and interest in these organizations seemed to decrease in parallel. Nevertheless, a few studies were devoted to them. This was the case in the UK (McRobie et al., 1957) and in the US where their role in corporate research activities was emphasized (Batelle Memorial Institute, 1956). In some countries, when the state remained interventionist in the economy, their role was unique. In France, for example, to control inflation, the state practiced continuous control over prices, albeit with fluctuations (price freezes followed by periods of semi-liberalization). The negotiation of prices with the public administration was one of the main and important activities of French trade associations (Dumez & Jeunemaître, 1989). In Japan, the Ministry of Economy, Trade and Industry (METI) steered industrial policy in liaison with trade associations, in particular because of the shortages of raw materials that had to be split between sectors. The integration between METI's administrative services and trade associations was almost fusional:

> It is difficult, and perhaps not useful, to attempt to define the boundary between government and business in any given major business decision. (Abegglen, 1970, p. 72)

Interest in the collective action of firms and the devices that organize it was renewed in the 1980s, precisely because of the economic relations between Japan, a major exporter, and Western countries.

TRADE ASSOCIATIONS IN THE US AND JAPAN IN THE 1980S

In the 1980s, collective action became a topic for reflection at the political and economic levels, particularly with the work of Philippe Schmitter and Wolfgang Streeck (Schmitter & Streeck, 1999; Streeck & Schmitter, 1985a, 1985b). Streeck and Schmitter spoke of a "corporate-associative order ... based primarily on interaction between complex organizations" (Streeck & Schmitter, 1985b, p. 124). On the industrial front, many Western industries were in crisis because of cheap imports. This was the case with textiles, steel, and automobiles, for example. US companies banded together to bring antidumping actions before the US Department of Commerce and the International Trade Commission. More generally, they denounced cartels organized by Japanese firms and supported by METI. For example, the American Iron and Steel Institute set up an international trade committee that met once a month. This committee created task forces on special subjects. It was in continuous contact with US authorities (Department of Commerce, International Trade Commission, State Department, and U.S. Trade Representative). When the committee had developed a common position, it was communicated to the government relations committee that that oversaw lobbying. As a first step, American producers demanded protective tariffs, but when they realized that the system would be difficult to set up they demanded import quotas. Economic liberalism based on mistrust of collective action between firms was then strongly criticized. Industrialists argued for more cooperation and, for example, in 1984 the National Cooperative Research and Production Act was adopted, a US federal law that reduces potential antitrust liabilities of research joint ventures and standards development organizations.

In 1988, two researchers, Leonard H. Lynn and Timothy J. McKeown, investigated for the American Enterprise Institute the comparative role of trade associations in Japan and the US. They focused their comparison on two sectors, the iron and steel industry and machine tools. On the political and macroeconomic level, their thesis was that a relative convergence was taking place. American economic liberalism was tempered, as the passing of the National Cooperative Research and Production Act showed. On the Japanese side, the close ties between the METI and the trade associations were loosening. On the one hand, Japanese companies had become international-ized and therefore less dependent on the Japanese state. On the other hand, the Japan Fair Trade Commission had acquired more power and it began to attack cartels (in 1991, for example, two cartels in the cement sector were con-demned – Nihon Cement and Onoda Cement; Dumez & Jeunemaître, 2000; Tilton, 1996). Extending Naylor's study, the study led by Lynn and McKeown deepened the analysis of trade associations. It also illustrated the difficulty of comparing the role of this type of organization in two different political and economic systems and the difficulty of understanding the effect of the political and economic action of these associations.

Evolution and Roles of Meta-organizations

Remember that Naylor provided a first definition of trade associations:

> A trade association is an organization for the mutual benefits of individuals or com-panies who are engaged in the same kind of business. (Naylor, 1921, p. 3)

Lynn and McKeown provided a new one:

> Trade associations may be defined as nonprofit membership organizations whose members are primarily business firms rather than individuals and which perform a variety of activities for their member firms. (Lynn & McKeown, 1988, p. 6)

We see that this new definition by Lynn and McKeown emphasized an important evolution – the fact that the members of trade associations were at that time mainly firms, that is, organizations. Individual members had disappeared from the definition. Even if the term used by Ahrne and Brunsson (2005, 2008) – meta-organization – did not yet exist, the trade associations had become organizations whose members are organizations, that is to say, the definition given by Ahrne and Brunsson (2005, 2008). Lynn and McKeown identified the main activities of these organizations:

1. Product promotion: promoting sales of the industry's products – most commonly, advertising or using other communications tools to increase customer awareness, or holding trade shows
2. Labor relations: monitoring labor agreements in the industry; providing consulting and technical services relating to collective bargaining; conducting wage and benefit surveys
3. Standard setting: working with private or public agencies to develop product or process standards for the industry; developing an industry position and then ensuring that the position is enacted
4. Data collection: compiling statistics from member firms or from other sources (such as government agencies) on industry production, sales, capacity utilization, and imports and exports, and providing members with this information
5. Research and development: performing or funding R&D; disseminating technical information to members and, when deemed appropriate, to customers or others
6. Economic services to firms: offering group buying plans, group insurance, member discounts on various products, special member prices for consulting or technical services, credit bureaus, and collection services
7. Educational services: preparing seminars, audio-visual materials, printed matter pertaining to just about any subject which may be germane to successful operations in the industry in question
8. Conventions and general membership meetings
9. Public relations (often closely related to government relations or to product promotion) (Lynn & McKeown, 1988, p. 3)

This was the broad range of services that a business meta-organization could provide, which Lyn Spillman has called the "multifunctional portfolio of goals and activities" (Spillman, 2012, p. 106). This range appeared very stable over time. A particular trade association usually had several activities in this range, but not all of them, and the activities it carried out could evolve over time. This was also the case in Japan as in the US:

> Associations select differently from a range of activities characteristic of the institution as a whole, and they may change their focus over time. (Spillman, 2012, p. 13)

From these common characteristics of meta-organizations in Japan and the US, Lynn and McKeown compared their role and operation in both countries.

The Japan–US Comparison

The chronologies were quite parallel. We have seen that the major American trade associations were born in the late nineteenth century. In the same way, the Japanese banks created a trade association in 1876 and the first industrial trade association appeared in 1880 – the Japan Paper Manufacturing Federation – followed in 1882 by the Japan Cotton Spinners' Association. The comparison of the size of trade associations in Japan and the US did not lead to the identification of significant differences between the two countries. In terms of number of permanent employees, most American trade associations had around five to ten permanent employees. Many Japanese trade associations had less than five permanent staff. From this point of view, the American Iron and Steel Institute was a big organization for the US (66 permanent members of staff) but its Japanese counterpart, the Japan Iron and Steel Federation, was even more important (170 permanent members of staff). In the case of the machine tool industry, the US National Machine Tool Builders' Association was much larger (60 permanent members of staff for 400 affiliated firms) than its Japanese counterpart, the Machine Tool Builders' Association (12 permanent members of staff for 112 affiliated firms). In both countries, trade associations had organized joint research actions:

> Trade associations in both the United States and Japan have frequently provided their members with important services related to technology: giving them information on new technological developments, conducting research on their behalf, and on occasion receiving government research subsidies for them. These activities have, however, tended to be more constant and more intensive in Japan than in the United States. (Lynn & McKeown, 1988, p. 140)

Similarly, one of their core activities was foreign trade and especially exports:

> A common and important role for trade associations in both the United States and Japan has been the promotion of exports for member firms and the protection of local markets against foreign competitors. These activities have intensified in recent years. (Lynn & McKeown, 1988, p. 120)

Nevertheless, with the internationalization of companies and the beginning of globalization, the situation began to evolve. With mergers and alliances, Japanese firms became members of American trade associations and vice versa. As a result, the role of trade associations in trade policies became more problematic: it became more difficult for an American trade association to promote the fight against Japanese imports when some of their members were Japanese-owned firms operating in the US.

In both countries there were also collective action problems and conflicts between firms and meta-organizations. The chief executive officer (CEO) of Wheeling-Pittsburgh Steel Corporation officially opposed the American Iron and Steel Institute in 1983. In 1965, the Japan Iron and Steel Federation set up a special committee to control investments in new steel mills. The METI supported the initiative, without being legally empowered to do so and set investment quotas, which it divided into 85 firms. The company Sumitomo considered it an illegal decision that interfered with its decision-making autonomy and refused to comply with the quota it had been allocated. The METI decided to reduce Sumitomo's coal import quota. Before this measure came into force, demand for steel rose again and an agreement was reached (Kaplan, 1972, pp. 147–8). Low exit costs accounted for this potential instability of meta-organizations. Probably for political reasons, they were weaker in the US than in Japan:

> The fact that U.S. firms can often leave their association at relatively low cost if the association takes policy positions with which they disagree no doubt limits the extent to which associations take policy positions. (Lynn & McKeown, 1988, p. 56)

What differences were there between trade associations in the US and Japan? In the US, the end of World War II was characterized by a sharp decline in the interventionism of the federal state and thus a lesser role for business meta-organizations. In Japan, they continued to play the role they had during the war economy long after the end of World War II because of shortages of raw materials. For Japan, the war began in China in 1937. From that time, the economy was organized by the state and it was based on organizations representing different sectors of the economy. Contrary to what Mancur Olson (1982) might have thought, even though they changed their name, these trade associations and the personnel who worked for them continued to operate between 1945 and the 1980s. In the cement sector, for example, the Japan Cement Association was created in February 1948 to replace the Japan Cement Industry Association by inheriting much of its staff (Fujii, 1948). The Japanese political system gave meta-organizations a prominent place. Throughout the period, the same political party (Liberal-Democratic Party) retained the majority, with the same people remaining in power in government, in ministries, and in companies. The links were very close and trade associations often hired former public servants (for example, in March 1984, the Cement Association hired Ono Masabumi, a former METI official; Tilton, 1996). The trade associations then played a decisive role on two interconnected levels. For geographical, cultural, and linguistic reasons, Japanese industry had no export tradition. Nor did it have a great tradition of product quality. When it made its first attempts to export, Japanese products were considered in Western countries of extremely poor quality. This was the case, for example, for cars. The trade associations managed to standardize and control much of the quality, to the point that the image of Japan changed completely in a few decades – from being poor-quality products, Japanese products became the reference point for high quality, much superior to the products of American or European industries:

> Through export associations and other organizations loosely affiliated with the trade associations and backed by law, it was possible to impose quality standards that would make it easier to sell Japanese products in general. (Lynn & McKeown, 1988, p. 135)

In parallel, in association with the METI, the Japanese trade associations gathered information and supported Japanese companies in their export development:

> The major postwar association for steel producers and traders, the Kozai Club, was quick to help Japanese steelmakers identify and move to export markets. It began making overseas market surveys in 1949, collecting, compiling, and distributing reports and information from Europe and North America. A Japanese university professor sent back reports from Antwerp, Belgium, on developments in Europe. In 1950, the Kozai Club began publishing periodicals on the iron industry in Europe, the United States, and other countries. It began collecting major foreign trade journals and by the mid-1950s was producing specialized reports on aspects of the economic environment of the steel industry in foreign countries. Japanese studies in the early 1960s took up labor-management relations in the U.S. steel industry, U.S. market structures, trade, and other topics to give Japanese industry officials more information on U.S. attitudes and policies regarding dumping. (Lynn & McKeown, 1988, p. 129)

This strategy of Japanese trade associations was systematic and continuous. But in the 1980s, as has been stated, Japan's political and economic system came closer to that of other countries. Government alternated between political parties, the METI lost power over the Japan Fair Trade Commission, Japanese companies became more international and less dependent on the state. Were there then Japanese specificities in trade associations? Lynn and McKeown remained cautious in their analysis but they found some interesting points.

Industrial sectors had a complex structure in both Japan and the US. In the iron and steel sector in the US, there was, of course, the American Iron and Steel Institute, but also 45 other associations. In total, the structure was quite "messy." In Japan, the same diversity was found but the structure was more hierarchical and integrative:

> The system approximates a hierarchy in which each level aggregates and reconciles the interests represented at that level. (Lynn & McKeown, 1988, p. 81)

Integration was facilitated by the fact that often the different associations for the same sector shared the same building, which facilitated coordination. This was the case in iron and steel and it was also the case in the machine tool industry. The Machinery Promotion Building (Kikai Shinko Kaikan), built in 1966, was shared by the Japan Machine Tool Builders' Association, the Japan Machinery Federation, the Japan Society for the Promotion of the Machinery Industry, and the Machine Tool and Related Products Committee. But the difference between Japan and USA seemed to take place especially at the level of information management:

> Japanese trade associations and related organizations have given more attention than their American counterparts to collecting and providing access to foreign technical information. Japanese trade associations frequently provide Japanese language abstracts of technical articles, organize overseas study trips, and keep files of materials on foreign companies and products. They also seem to have been more apt to consider this activity, along with the purchase of foreign equipment and products, as a legitimate part of their collaborative research effort. American associations generally lag behind their Japanese counterparts in these activities. (Lynn & McKeown, 1988, p. 167)

So, it was not so much the collaborative research that seemed to make the difference. We saw that the US had adopted in 1984 an act allowing collaborative research and that, in any case, American trade associations had been practicing this since the beginning of the twentieth century. Rather, it was Japan's information management, dealing with markets and technology:

> Japanese industry has frequently assigned important roles to its trade associations in areas where American industry does not. A prominent example is their activity in the collection of information about foreign technology and foreign markets. (Lynn & McKeown, 1988, p. 175)

On the US side, the trade associations were more oriented towards public communication and political action:

> During 1980 the five most frequent "public policy" advertisers were all trade associations.[6] A survey by Industrial Marketing reported that companies supported such association efforts for two reasons: "One, the expense needed to even dent public opinion is staggering. Two, more than a few ... companies have some serious credibility problems because of ... years of bad press." Association ads give companies "more bang for the buck:" the pooling of expenditures makes an association campaign to influence public policy much more attractive than a campaign led by a firm of a few hundred employees. (Lynn & McKeown, 1988, p. 106)

In Japan, the influence of industrial sectors on political power appeared to be great, but it went through more direct and informal channels.

In total, the Lynn and McKeown study illustrates several points. The role of trade associations depends on the political-economic system in which they operate. When these systems are substantially different, comparisons are difficult. Indeed, the risk is to compare apples with oranges (Locke & Thelen, 1995). Spillman (2012) emphasizes the cultural dimension of trade associations. This dimension exists, but the political and economic nature of the system in which they operate seems to us more important. For example, in Japan from 1945 to the 1980s, the political-economic system was characterized by strong state interventionism. The services of the METI and trade associations took joint decisions even though, as we have seen, some problems of collective action appeared. Then, with the internationalization of Japanese companies, with the rise of the Japanese Fair Trade Commission, Japan moved closer to the political and economic systems of other democratic countries. Since then, the role and functions of trade associations have become commonplace, to the point of resembling what happens in other countries. The second crucial point is that it is very difficult to assess the political and economic impact of trade associations. At the level of their size and structure, the American and Japanese trade associations seem not to be vastly different. They perform the same functions overall. To understand their respective impact, it is necessary to analyze their operation in detail, which is methodologically difficult. Presented with caution, Lynn and McKeown's results are that Japanese trade associations were able to operate in a more hierarchical and organized way than their American counterparts and, above all, had better collected, processed, and disseminated information and knowledge on the technology and markets than US trade associations. They were able to advance the Japanese industry in terms of quality and help to export and internationalize.

NEW TRENDS CONCERNING FCADS

As we have seen, most of the characteristics of today's business meta-organizations were present at the beginning of the twentieth century (collection, processing, and dissemination of information, lobbying, action on CSR, services to members, joint research, etc.). Is there anything new in the recent period?

The Emergence of New Types of Business Associations

In addition to traditional trade associations, representing an industry or several industries and assuming some or all the functions identified by Lynn and McKeown, other types of collective action devices have appeared since the 1960s (Bastianutti & Dumez, 2018; Berkowitz & Dumez, 2015; Berkowitz, Bucheli & Dumez, 2017). These were first specialized business meta-organizations (Barnett & King, 2008; Berkowitz et al., 2017). For example, in the petroleum industry, the CONservation of Clean Air and Water in Europe (CONCAWE) was created in 1963 on the initiative of a small group of firms in the sector. Its objective is "to improve scientific understanding of the environmental health, safety and economic performance aspects of both petroleum refining and the distribution and sustainable use of refined products." Traditional trade associations were organized into internal, permanent, or transitional committees, and some of them had established research laboratories. From the 1960s, it was as if some of these committees or laboratories were transformed into autonomous meta-organizations. In the 2000s, another type of device appeared – multistakeholder meta-organizations, meta-organizations whose members are at the same time firms, states, NGOs, and other actors such as universities. In 2000, for example, the Voluntary Principles on Security and Human Rights (VPSHR) initiative was created, whose members are the major multinational extractive companies (oil and gas and mining), governments, and NGOs. At the end of the twentieth century, various collective action schemes emerged in the form of meta-organizations. They can be grouped around three dimensions: the level, the issue treated, and their members, shown in Table 2.1 (see overleaf).

The FCADs in Table 2.1 take the following form:

- Specialized meta-organization at an infra-sectoral level (e.g., business club): a group of firms belonging to one sector creates a specialized meta-organization to focus on a problem common to the sector.
- Specialized meta-organization at the sectoral level: all the firms in a sector create a specialized meta-organization focused on a social or environ-

mental problem (as if an internal committee of the trade association was transformed into an autonomous organization).
• Specialized meta-organization at a supra-sectoral level: several industrial sectors concerned by a problem create a meta-organization devoted to this problem.
• Specialized meta-organization at a cross-sectoral level (multi-industry business club): a group of firms belonging to various sectors creates a meta-organization devoted to a problem common to these different companies.
• Multistakeholder meta-organization: companies, governments, and NGOs jointly create a meta-organization to solve a problem.

Table 2.1   *The diversity of firms' collective action devices*

Level	Issue	Members	Example(s)
Infra-sectoral	A problem inside the industry	A group of firms in the industry	CSI
Sectoral	A social or environmental problem	All firms in the industry	CONCAWE
Supra-sectoral	A problem concerning many industries in the same branch	Industrial sectors	EEB, SBCI
Cross-sectoral	A problem concerning some firms in non-related industries	A group of firms from different industries	GBI
With stakeholders	A social or environmental problem	Firms, public authorities, NGOs, etc.	UNGC, VPSHR

Note: CONCAWE = CONservation of Clean Air and Water in Europe; CSI = Cement Sustainability Initiative; EEB = Energy Efficiency in Buildings; GBI = Global Business Initiative; SBCI = Sustainable Building and Construction Initiative; UNGC = United Nations Global Compact; VPSHR = Voluntary Principles on Security and Human Rights.

In practice, firms are members of traditional meta-organizations, that is, trade associations (in all countries where they operate, and sometimes at supranational level – European, for example) and chambers of commerce, while being also members of new forms of meta-organizations. In the 2000s, the cement group Lafarge belonged, for example, to a multitude of meta-organizations. The first were, of course, the national trade associations of the cement industry (the Portland Cement Association in the US, the Syndicat Français de l'Industrie Cimentière in France, etc.). But Lafarge was also a member of a business club it co-created with its competitor Holcim in the cement industry, the Cement Sustainability Initiative (CSI). At an intersectoral level, which brings together all the industries involved in building, Lafarge was a member of Energy Efficiency in Buildings (EEB) and Sustainable Building and Construction Initiative (SBCI). At a cross-sectoral level, Lafarge belonged to the World Business Council for Sustainable Development (WBCSD) and the Global Business Coalition (GBC), a business club fighting the spread of HIV (Bastianutti & Dumez, 2018).

How to explain this proliferation of forms of meta-organizations between 1960 and the 2000s? Two factors played a role. On the one hand, an area of accountability has been structured to change the behavior of companies regarding a set of problems that have been grouped under the concept of CSR. Trade associations have (re-)entered the field of CSR and sustainable development (Buchanan, 2016; Djelic & den Hond, 2014; Marques, 2017). On the other hand, there has been a profound change in the form of law in the recent period.

The Field of Responsibilizing Corporations

David Vogel (2005) spoke of a market of virtue on which companies would operate from now on. Rather than a market, it may be more appropriate to speak of a field of responsibilization (Bastianutti & Dumez, 2012). Because of the complexity of their organizational nature, the complexity and diversity of the environment in which they operate, companies are in a state of organizational hypocrisy (Brunsson, 2003; Dumez, 2012): the discourses they hold can vary and their practices often do not correspond to their speeches. Moral entrepreneurs (Becker, 1995), often NGOs, defend various specialized causes (gender equality, animal welfare, air or water pollution, working conditions, etc.). They shine a spotlight on the differences between the speeches and the practices of the firms and give them a microphone, summoning them to explain themselves (Van Parijs, 2002). Jon Elster (1998) spoke about the civilizing force of hypocrisy based on the existence of a public space. The field thus consists of potential conflicts between moral entrepreneurs, supported by experts, and firms. A firm announcing an action plan remains suspect in the field and vulnerable to further attacks. It is better for it to place its reputation under the umbrella of the collective reputation of a group of firms:

> [Companies] can also protect themselves from the skepticism and incredulity that might arise from, for example, a Hooker Chemical Company ad on responsible chemical waste disposal. (Frederick & Myers, 1983, p. 70)

Let's look at a case. In the 1990s, journalists and NGOs attacked Nike about working conditions at some of its suppliers in Southeast Asia. On the legal side, Nike was not responsible for the local management of production operations in its supply network, but in the field, it was a potential target (Levy, 2008). In 1999, Nike cofounded the Fair Labor Association, a multistakeholder meta-organization that brought together companies, universities, and human rights and labor representatives to establish independent controls and a code of conduct.

The field of responsibilization has evolved. The points of tension between the company and society have shifted. At the end of the nineteenth century, the traditional forms of the business meta-organization, that is, the trade association and the chamber of commerce, constituted the collective response of companies to the problems they faced at the time: the emergence of trade unions and the commercial issues (tariffs). The current forms of business meta-organizations are the collective response of contemporary companies to the forms of organizing of moral entrepreneurs (NGOs) operating in human rights, the environment, and all subjects constituting sustainable development. They are specialized because the moral entrepreneurs themselves are generally specialized in a cause to promote (known as "category killers"). But another factor played a role in the evolution of business meta-organizations – the evolution of the law.

The Evolution of Law

Traditional law is based on the formulation of prohibitions (smoking is prohibited) or prescriptions (you must respect the speed limit), but new types of rules have emerged and multiplied in recent years (Westerman, 2018). These rules state that a desirable objective must be achieved, as is the case, for example, with the European Commission's framework directives, which often relate to the environment or sustainable development. Take the following case:

> The marine environment is a precious heritage that must be protected, preserved and, where practicable, restored with the ultimate aim of maintaining biodiversity and providing diverse and dynamic oceans and seas which are clean, healthy and productive. (Commission Decision 2008/56/EC, Marine Strategy Framework Directive; European Commission, 2008)

We often speak of "principles-based regulation," but the expression is misleading – the principles are general, but these regulations can be extremely detailed. The difference from the classic rules is elsewhere. The new rules no longer bear the means, but the ends. Fuller wrote that law was the emptiest of sciences, "all means and no end" (Fuller, 1968, pp. 10–11). Here, there is a reversal: these rules are "all ends and no means" (Westerman, 2018, p. 4).

Rather than as a retreat of the state (Strange, 1996), it is in this sense that we must understand the notion of outsourcing of law:

> a ... radical practice in which the outsourcer *confines* herself to formulating the desired outcomes or end-states ("the what") leaving it to the outsourcees to formulate the "how": the means by which these goals can be reached. (Westerman, 2018, p. 5; original emphasis)

Those who will do the work (the outsourcees) may be private or public in nature. Increasing numbers of actors are involved in the formulation of the rules. The new rules still have the same structure, which is found in many laws passed at the national level. The structure is tripartite. First, the wording of an aspiration: an objective is declared important. Then there is a rule of implementation: the obligation to put in place a device that will achieve the desired goal. Finally, a standard of accountability: the need to make reports showing progress in moving towards the defined goal. The implemented process proceeds by concretization and specification. The objective formulated in a very general way is broken down into sub-objectives. It is thus concretized. Then, indicators are assigned to each sub-goal: this is the specification. Outsourcing of law is characterized by an "inherent tendency towards differentiation and proliferation of both rules and organizations" (Westerman, 2018, p. 49). Specific, measurable, assignable, realistic, time-related (SMART; Doran, 1981) indicators need to be developed, with detailed reporting and accountability rules. Government departments delegate this work to organizations closest to the activities concerned by the rules – mainly to meta-organizations. Contemporary business meta-organizations are today one of the essential organizational supports for the evolution of the rules. They provide expertise on the indicators and on the accountability and reporting rules they are defining and operating.

CONCLUSION

It is difficult to build an overall historical vision of collective action devices set up by firms. Nevertheless, some salient features of their dynamics appear. The two prototypical devices are the trade association (bringing together firms from the same sector, even if the concept of sector is vague) and the chamber of commerce (bringing together firms from different sectors). These two devices are surprisingly stable over time: they appeared at the end of the eighteenth century, developed in the nineteenth, became meta-organizations at the beginning of the twentieth century, that is to say, organizations whose members are organizations (and no longer individuals) with permanent staff. They are surprisingly stable. The activities they perform today were already present at the beginning of the twentieth century. These devices are found in all countries and internationally. The recent period is characterized by the emergence of new organizational forms that have developed outside the sector (subsectoral, supra-sectoral, cross-sectoral) or with stakeholders (multistakeholder meta-organizations).

CHAPTER SUMMARY

Business meta-organizations appeared in the nineteenth century as chambers of commerce in response to questions of international trade and as trade associations in response to labor organizations. They became true organizations – with an office and a permanent secretary – at the turn of the twentieth century. As early as the 1920s, trade associations presented their characteristic features with a well-defined set of functions: negotiations with public authorities, influence on parliaments, collection, processing and dissemination of information, provision of services to their members, organization of collective research, and so on. As early as the 1920s, antitrust jurisprudence was fairly well established: these FCADs knew what kind of information they could collect, process, and disseminate, and what types of competitive behavior were prohibited. Their organization into permanent and transitional committees allowed them great flexibility: depending on the period, they could focus on lobbying on tariffs, or on stimulating exports, price negotiations (in price control periods), wage negotiations, and so on. This plasticity probably explains their stability:

> Of associations existing in 2003 [in the US], 21 percent had been founded before 1940, and over a third (38 percent) before 1960, another indicator of the stability of the organizational population. (Spillman, 2012, p. 87)

In the recent period, organizational creativity has been added to plasticity with the invention of new organizational forms: instead of creating new internal committees within trade associations, firms have created autonomous specialized meta-organizations at the sector level, at the level of several related sectors, at an infra- or cross-sectoral level. Multistakeholder meta-organizations have also appeared, whose members are firms, but also states, NGOs, or universities. This evolution is due to two joint factors. While the role of trade unions has weakened, firms have come up against new problem-oriented organizations – NGOs as moral entrepreneurs. The firms then responded with meta-organizations also specialized in various topics related to CSR, sustainable development, human rights, and so on. It turns out that, at the same time, these topics are those for which there is an evolution of the form of the rules. The traditional rules of law that force or prohibit are giving way to rules that set general objectives that are then translated into target indicators, with accountability and reporting procedures on how these indicators are met or not. This way of elaborating rules and monitoring their implementation is based on specialized organizations of the meta-organization type.

NOTES

1. Ludwig Wittgenstein's philosophical idea of family resemblance (*Familienähnlichkeit*) is described in his posthumously published book *Philosophical Investigations* (1953 [2008]). It argues that things that could be thought to be connected by one essential common feature may in fact be connected by a series of overlapping similarities, where no one feature is common to all.
2. Goldsmiths, gilders, and butchers' streets, respectively.
3. See Chapter 3.
4. In France, for example, it would take almost a century for the French Revolution's ban on collective structures to be repealed (Waldeck-Rousseau Act of 1884).
5. As was the case in the United Kingdom, as we have seen, with, for example, the cotton industry in the middle of the eighteenth century.
6. The American Gas Association, the American Council on Life Insurance, the Chemical Manufacturers' Association, the American Insurance Association, and the Association of American Railroads (Frederick & Myers, 1983, pp. 69–70).

3.   On political and economic problems raised by business meta-organizations

In the eighteenth century, both the political philosophy of democracy and the theory of political economy were formed. Both condemned economic interest groups. In political philosophy, they were perceived as "factions", the term being extremely pejorative. As noticed by Streeck and Schmitter (1985a, p. 3), "associations have always been regarded much more as a source of disorder [than of social order]." In the theory of political economy, they were suspected of impeding the free market by setting prices and controlling the quantities produced and sold. The industrial and democratic societies of the nineteenth century tended to ban them. They were eventually allowed but remain a problem within the political and economic framework of contemporary societies.

ORIGINS AND FORMULATION OF THE POLITICAL PROBLEM

In January 1789 in France, in the context of the preparation process of the États généraux (States General legislative assembly), thousands of copies of a political pamphlet written by the Abbé Emmanuel Joseph Sieyès, *Qu'est-ce que le tiers état?* (What is the Third State?), sold in a just a few weeks. It was to mark the spirit of the times and played an important role in the revolutionary events that were to follow. In the pamphlet, we find these reflections:

> Personal interest is not to be feared; it is isolated, everyone has his own; the great difficulty comes from the interest by which a citizen agrees with only a few others. This allows one work together, to gang up. Through it dangerous projects for the community are combined, through it the most formidable public enemies are formed. So let's not be surprised then if the social order so vigorously demands not to let private citizens have corporations.[1]

The French Revolution effectively abolished the *"corporations"* in 1789 (Soubiran-Paillet, 1993) through the d'Allarde Law (2–17 March 1791) and

Le Chapelier Law (14 June 1791). In his speech to the assembly, Le Chapelier said:

> No doubt all citizens should be allowed to assemble; but citizens of certain profes-
> sions should not be permitted to assemble for their so-called common interests; there
> is no longer a corporation in the state; there is only the particular interest of each
> individual, and the general interest. No one is permitted to inspire citizens with an
> intermediary interest, to separate them from the public good by a corporate spirit.[2]

And again:

> no society, club, association of citizens can have in any form a political existence,
> nor exert any action or inspection on the acts of the constituted powers and the legal
> authorities ... under any pretext, they will not be able to appear under a collective
> name ... to form petitions or deputations.[3]

A few years earlier, American revolutionaries had raised the same question in the *Federalist Papers* Nos 9 ("The Union as a Safeguard Against Domestic Faction and Insurrection") and 10 ("The Same Subject Continued: The Union as a Safeguard Against Domestic Faction and Insurrection"), the first by Alexander Hamilton and the second by James Madison (both in 1787). It was Madison who had actually verbalized the problem. For him, the appearance of factions in a free political space was inevitable – factions have their roots in human nature and in an unequal distribution of property. He defines them in the following way:

> By a faction I understand a number of citizens, whether amounting to a majority or
> a minority of the whole, who are united and actuated by some common impulse of
> passion, or of interest, adverse to the rights of other citizens, or to the permanent and
> aggregate interests of the community. (Madison, *Federalist Papers*, No. 10)

For Madison, protection against factions is offered by a certain transparency of the decision-making process within a republic and by the size of society that produces a multitude of intermediary bodies that can neutralize each other. Classical political thought, notably Montesquieu, which greatly inspired the American constituents, considered that the republican regime suited only small societies like the Athenian city. Madison, breaking this point with Montesquieu, thinks that the republic, on the contrary, is adaptable to large states precisely because it is the only regime that can neutralize the inevitable factions that cannot fail to appear in such situations (Conniff, 1975).

In fact, it was Rousseau who best analyzed the problem.[4] He wrote in 1762 in *The Social Contract* (Book II, Chapter 3):

It is therefore important, in order to have a clear statement of the general will, that there is no partial society in the state, and that every citizen should only opine according to himself ... If there were partial societies, we must multiply their number and prevent inequality ... These precautions are the only good so that the general will is always enlightened and the people are not mistaken.[5]

Four fundamental propositions are found in this short text and they perfectly express the nature of the political problem posed by the organizations in charge of defending private interests:

- Private interests forming in associations or organizations may threaten the collective interest, the general will.
- It is likely that in a free society the formation of these associations is inevitable.
- If this is the case, then they must be as numerous as possible.
- This condition is not in itself sufficient; they must also be on the best possible level of equality – that some are significantly more powerful than others must be avoided.

The work of Olson (1965) has shown that collective action is much easier to organize for small groups than for large groups where the phenomenon of free riding can be massive. Therefore, meta-organizations are easier to create and appeared earlier on the supply side of markets (i.e., business meta-organizations) than on the demand side. Structurally, it is easier to create and operate a meta-organization when it represents 100 firms in a sector than an organization aiming to represent the millions of consumers. Therefore, because of their inequalities of power, even if the representative organizations (trade associations) are multiple in society, it is illusory to think that this multiplicity guarantees a kind of global balance:

Some types of groups form more easily than others, so that the interest group environment is not always, or even perhaps ever, in equilibrium. Thus, while it may not be the case that a single elite dominates all American politics, neither is it true that all groups are equally represented and have equal resources to engage in politics. (Berry & Wilcox, 2018, p. 11)

Even within the population of trade associations representing the actors of a sector, there are strong inequalities. 77 percent of US trade associations have less than 12 permanent staff (Spillman, 2012). In the UK, 73 percent of trade associations have less than five permanent employees. However, it can be hypothesized that effective long-term lobbying, involving close contacts with politicians and officials, requires substantial staffing. From this point of view, the inequalities between groups are great. Studying American trade associations, Spillman finds the following phenomenon:

> [J]ust under a third of associations are headquartered in the DC area.[6] These associations tend to be composed of firms, and to have more staff and committees. (Spillman, 2012, p. 272)

Similarly, meta-organizations are more likely to lobby than professional associations whose members are individual firms and which are more public relations oriented. Galambos (1966) speaks of triocracies: in the different areas of state intervention, decisions are taken jointly by interest groups (mainly business meta-organizations), parliamentarians, and government agencies. Once relational investment is made, the business meta-organization benefits from an inertial access ("previous access establishes the basis for future access"; Oberman, 2008, p. 254). From there, it can directly influence political decision-making, that is, engage in lobbying:

> Although lobbying conjures up the image of an interest group representative trying to persuade a legislator to vote in the group's favor, we should see it in a broader context. Lobbying can be directed at any branch of government – legislative, judicial, or executive. Interest groups can even try to influence those institutions indirectly by attempting to sway public opinion, which they hope in turn will influence government. (Berry & Wilcox, 2018, pp. 6–7)

Lobbying can take many forms (bringing a lawsuit, trying to influence journalists or politicians, etc.). Just about any legal means used to try to influence government can be called lobbying. The first influence that business meta-organizations can have on policy-makers is that of agenda-setting, which is directly related to lobbying:

> A related activity is *agenda building* ... interest groups are frequently responsible for bringing the issue to light in the first place. The world has many problems, but not all are political issues being actively considered by government. Agenda building turns problems into issues, which become part of the body of policy questions that government feels it must deal with. (Berry & Wilcox, 2018, p. 8; original emphasis)

Agenda building recovers both formal and procedural, informal and substantive agenda-setting, the latter being the field of policy entrepreneurs (Pollack, 1997). But then, lobbying can go further and articulate several actions:

- to influence the creation of a law or regulation in the favor of an organization;
- to amend the characteristics or impact of a proposed law or regulation in favor of an organization;

- to revise or review the interpretation or implementation of a law or regulation in favor of an organization;
- to understand how change as a product of a law or regulation affects an organization;
- to manage perceptions of change to create a favorable impression of your organization. (Baines & Viney, 2010, p. 262)

Coleman (1985) identifies two roles of "interest associations" or interest groups: policy advocacy and policy participation. The aim of policy advocacy is to defend the interests of the members, and only these. The group's activity can therefore compete with and be detrimental to other social groups, organized or unorganized. It mainly consists of exchanges of information with the state. Then, policy participation consists of aggregating the information exchanged. Here, the challenge for the meta-organization is to have an added value, to show to its members, the state, and, more broadly, the society that the association is more than the sum of the interests of its members. This poses a problem of rationality (therefore an economic problem) to meta-organizations:

> As interest associations, trade associations are subject to the collective rationality problem in that their survival depends not only on how well they represent membership interests, but also on how effectively they aggregate the parochial preferences of their members. (Lippmann & Aldrich, 2016, p. 663)

All these actions do not always appear in the open, but others are more visible. During the 1980 US presidential campaign that opposed Jimmy Carter and Ronald Reagan, among the ten most frequent advertisers in *Business Week*, *Newsweek*, and *The Atlantic* the top five were trade associations: American Gas Association, American Council of Life Insurance, Chemical Manufacturers' Association, American Insurance Association, and Association of American Railroads (Frederick & Myers, 1983, p. 69). The advertisements by these trade associations were quite directly in favor of Ronald Reagan, while the advertisements made by the individual companies were more neutral:

> One might therefore infer that the trade association as ad sponsor can be used by individual companies to get across a political message deemed to be too sensitive for direct linkage to a given corporation's name. (Frederick & Myers, 1983, p. 70)

Nank and Alexander (2012) mention the role of chambers of commerce in state-level judges' elections:

> Trade associations were used to influence judicial elections throughout several states as early as 1998. The Brennan Center for Justice generated by New York University Law School (2004) documented that judicial campaigns were targeted by the U.S. Chambers of Commerce seeking more "business friendly" judges on state Supreme

Courts. The Institute for Legal Reform (ILR), a trade association, was created and more than $5 million was invested in advertisements to influence judicial campaigns in Michigan, Mississippi, Ohio, Illinois and Alabama. The funding was intended to defeat incumbent judges who had ruled against companies that contributed to the U.S Chamber of Commerce. (Nank & Alexander, 2012, p. 451)

Hence, after Rousseau in 1762, here is a modern formulation of the political problem posed by business meta-organizations:

Can an acceptable balance be struck between the right of people to pursue their own interests and the need to protect society from being dominated by one or more interests? Can we achieve true pluralism, or is a severe imbalance of interest group power a chronic condition in a free and open society? Is the interest group universe today balanced, as the pluralists had hoped, or is it dominated by narrow groups seeking their own benefits at a cost to the larger society? (Berry & Wilcox, 2018, pp. 4–5)

That being said, the game is relational. The influence of business meta-organizations is all the stronger when the state that is supposed to develop the policy does not know which route to take:

The influence of trade associations, as of other interest groups, is strongest where the government has no clear-cut policy of its own. It is an illusion to suppose that there is some general public interest apart from the interest of the various sections of the community; but it is vital to remember that some sectional interests are badly organised and highly inarticulate – often, for instance, those of the final consumer. It is the responsibility of the Government and administration, therefore, to make up its own mind about industrial policy, and in doing so, to show especial concern for those interests which are less strongly organized. (McRobie et al., 1957, p. 255)

The starting point, therefore, is that of a government failure, since the state does not have the necessary knowledge to define the collective interest. The question is whether the definition of this collective interest proposed by the business meta-organizations reflects a democratic process, or only the expression of some particular interests that just manage to be heard more than others (the "iron law of oligarchy"; Michels, 1915). This political problem posed by the existence of highly organized interest groups is coupled with an economic problem.

THE ECONOMIC PROBLEM POSED BY FIRMS' COLLECTIVE ACTION

Why do some countries grow faster than others? And why does one country grow faster at certain periods and more slowly at others? Mancur Olson (1982) believes that the reason, probably not unique but decisive, is the existence of organized groups. He defends the idea that interest groups representing a marginal part of the economy can organize themselves effectively and weigh in on the political power to obtain measures (tariffs, subsidies, favorable tax measures, etc.) that provide them with long-term annuities to the detriment of the collective welfare. This is what we call rents of influence:

> Influence rents are the extra profits earned by an economic actor because the rules of the game of business are designed or changed to suit an economic actor or a group of economic actors. (Ahuja & Yayavaram, 2011, p. 1631)

These situations crystallize over time and acquire a form of irreversibility. Among the victors of World War II, they endured. In Germany and Japan, they were destroyed at the time of the defeat, which allowed these two economies to start again within a more favorable dynamic. The game of interest groups, and the most powerful of them business meta-organizations, has potentially three negative effects on the economy: (1) at the level of firms, resources are diverted to lobbying to try to create rents, resources that would be better employed in the productive sphere (seeking rents of influence instead of looking for gains in productivity and growth); (2) at the level of the economy as a whole, if rents are actually created, the resource allocation is no longer optimal; (3) dynamically, the production and diffusion of technological innovations are slowed down; not only is aggregate output less than it should be, but its growth rate is also lower than it should be (Wallerstein, 1984). This is because innovation that threatens certain interest groups can be delayed or blocked by them and because interest groups, paralyzed by their consensual decision-making process, are very slow to respond to new opportunities (König, Schulte & Enders, 2012). The status quo is becoming the most commonly accepted option and the creation of new industries, the adoption of new technologies, the adaptation to new environments are becoming increasingly difficult. When a society is stable, policy decisions become more complicated and politics focuses more on the redistribution of wealth between groups than on wealth creation and growth. Governments have been aware of the problem and have, from time to time, initiated studies on the potentially negative effects of trade associations, as was the case in the US in 1941 (Pearce, 1941) or in the UK in 1957 (McRobie et al., 1957).

Olson's analysis helps to understand why the two defeated countries of World War II, Germany and Japan, had very high growth rates, or why France grew faster than the UK postwar. Similarly, the period of stagflation, the combination not foreseen by the economic theory of inflation and unemployment, is explained by the fact that certain groups are able to block price reductions and protect their niches. Rebalancing can also take place between sectors, without directly involving the state, because of the action of business meta-organizations. Naylor already noted this in the 1920s in the comparative dynamics of the cement sector made up of a small number of well-organized firms, in relation to the dynamics of the timber sector made up of a very large number of small and medium-sized firms, which are so much harder to organize:

> By reason of the money that can be utilized "pooled" advertising, another name for association advertising, is always far more efficacious and wide-spread than individual advertising. The Portland Cement Association regularly expends hundreds of thousands of dollars a year merely in showing the advantages of good material and workmanship in roads, houses, farms, barns, walls, pig-pens, and all such buildings and construction work, as most people deal only with the medium of wood. (Naylor, 1921, p. 104)

Although Olson's approach can be based on this type of example, it has been strongly criticized. Indeed, the historical data mobilized are disparate and heterogeneous and their treatment lacks a rigorous econometric approach. Studying Japanese trade associations, as we have seen, Lynn and McKeown (1988) have shown, for example, that the thesis that they were destroyed at the end of the war was rather naive. In fact, many Japanese trade associations reformed in the immediate aftermath of the war by changing their names but ensuring a certain continuity, the leaders and staff of the old structures found themselves in the news. Following Olson's book, a multitude of other studies have been conducted on the subject. Many of them seem to confirm the hypothesis that the power of business meta-organizations can, at least in some cases, curb growth. At the same time, they have not led to widespread certainty (Heckelman, 2007). Bennett summarized the conclusion that can be drawn and nuanced:

> Associations are not necessarily a unique or even the most important aspect of the elements that explain differences in economic performance, but they can often play an important role. (Bennett, 1998, p. 1367)

The whole problem is to try to clarify this "can."

THE POLITICAL AND ECONOMIC INTEREST OF BUSINESS META-ORGANIZATIONS

That business meta-organizations can improve collective well-being because of better political decisions – the opposite of Olson's case – can also be argued. Several points can be highlighted. First, business meta-organizations can play a positive role in political decision-making. In modern economies, the state intervenes through multiple decisions. These decisions are risky – they can have great political or economic benefits or costs. However, to make these types of decision is expensive: it is necessary to consult all the actors who can be affected. If government agencies have to consult each of the firms in a sector, collect their opinion, try to reconcile opposing points of view for a regulatory decision, the cost – if only in time – will be extremely high. Having only one interlocutor, able to synthesize information and reach consensus, is welcomed by government agencies in their decision-making process, as has been noted for a long time:

> From the point of view of Government it is always a matter of great convenience to have a single consultative body for an industry. Sometimes the need for decision is urgent and time does not permit consultations with a great number of bodies or individual firms – a general view is required on short notice. Again, it is a great advantage for ministers and civil servants if differences of opinion in an industry can be reconciled inside an association before the question is brought before a department – the smaller the number of views the official has to deal with the simpler his task. (McRobie et al., 1957, pp. 66–7)

And:

> Trade associations are also an invaluable source of expert knowledge and advice on industrial matters. Ministries cannot be specialists in all branches and problems of industry. Associations, however, can and do provide up-to-date information on the needs of particular trades. Specifically, when trade negotiations with other countries, or a conference on countries working together under the GATT are about to take place, the Board of Trade consults the relevant associations on the proposals likely to be discussed. Similarly, all production departments consult the appropriate trade associations on proposed regulations and legislation. This two-way traffic of information and periodic exchange of views is of considerable value to public administrators, trade association officials and businessmen alike. Moreover, government departments can use some associations as a ready channel of communication with firms in particular lines of business; news about trade problems, new regulations, and business opportunities can conveniently be passed on to associations through bulletins or other types of trade publications. (McRobie et al., 1957, p. 67)

Second, once policy decisions are made, business meta-organizations can ensure some of the monitoring of regulation by lowering its costs (Bennett, 1998; Schmitter & Streeck, 1999; Streeck & Schmitter, 1985b) – for example, by pointing out to the public authorities the problems that the application of a regulation may give rise to, by organizing information meetings on the new regulations for their members, by publishing summary notes, by organizing exchanges on good practices, and so on. They can improve the competitiveness of firms in the sectors they represent by providing a range of services: joint research, specialized training, prospective studies, and so on. They can overcome market failures such as imperfect information, insufficient investment in training or lack of coordination in investment (Doner & Schneider, 2000). In addition, they can have a role to play in business development of countries, creating the conditions and institutions for economic growth, pushing underperforming states and obliging them to provide infrastructure, rules, and property rights that are necessary to a good performance of economy.

HOW TO ASSESS THE IMPACT OF BUSINESS META-ORGANIZATIONS?

Since the end of the eighteenth century, the effect of trade associations on political decisions and on the economy is the subject of debate. Positive and negative effects have been well identified, but the question of the repercussions of these effects arises. Evaluation is difficult in practice. Few studies have tried to solve the problem. Methodologically, it is necessary to choose a domain and to study it, as did Nank and Alexander (2012) and Laumann and Knoke (1987, 1988). Nank and Alexander showed how two trade associations were able to convince the state of Texas to develop coal electricity as the cleanest energy. Laumann and Knoke (1987, 1988) studied energy policy and health policy. The result of their research is enlightening. It will be remembered that Rousseau, and Madison in his wake, felt that democracy presupposed that the interest groups, if they appeared, were the numerous and the most diverse possible. On the contrary, Laumann and Knoke think that interest groups that have a real political weight are few and operate in a small number of areas with little connection between them. The world of political decision is a balkanized world:

> The norm of fighting for one's own interests but not against another's serves to reinforce a narrow vision of proper partisan conduct for most organizations. Even the environmental interest groups – which perceive dangers in many types of fuel usage – are highly selective in their attention to issues, in large measure because of the need to husband their resources. The result is a substantially balkanized domain structure, with a dozen or more subdomains in which most of the core organizations invest their resources. In the absence of a central subset of actors with diversified issue portfolios, the domain structure is better characterized as elite interest group pluralism rather than centralized coordination. (Laumann & Knoke, 1988, p. 22)

In these different areas, the interpenetration between the public sphere and the private sphere is very marked:

> The state is not a unitary actor, but a complex entity spanning multiple policy domains, comprised of both governmental organizations and those core private-sector participants whose interests must be taken into account. (Laumann & Knoke, 1988, p. 24)

It cannot be said that some interest groups representing some very well-organized economic sectors dominate the whole political decision. But, on the other hand, these interest groups, generally represented by business meta-organizations, can dominate an area of public action by isolating it from the rest of the public sphere:

> To the extent that political opinion is increasingly mediated by organizational activity within a variety of disjunctive policy domains, the concerns of easily organized interest groups will systematically be represented more effectively in policymaking processes.
>   This view of politics as systematically biased pluralist representation must be further modified. For, as has been made clear by the results of this research, the basis for effective political participation by organizations is not purely a product of the size of their constituencies but of their standing within those networks of organizations that have been labeled "policy domains." To the extent that this sort of dynamic prevails in national political life, policymaking is increasingly divorced or insulated from the expressed ideals of representative democracy. (Laumann & Knoke, 1988, p. 28)

Part of Olson's analysis is that groups that benefit from favorable conditions for collective action (small number of members) are organized and, having succeeded in isolating a field of public action, succeed in blurring the border between public sphere and private sphere by directing the public decision in the direction of their interest. On the other hand, it does not appear that organized groups are constantly dominant on multiple domains, which confirms Dahl's analyzes of the functioning of democracy: "Through negotiation and compromise between affected groups and political elites, democratic decisions are reached, with no one group consistently dominating" (Dahl, 1956, p. 145).

To understand the actual impact of meta-organizations on policy, perhaps the simplest and most conclusive approach is Wilson's (1973, p. 16; 1980). Wilson identifies policy cases from two dimensions: are the costs of this policy diffuse or concentrated? Are the benefits of this policy diffuse or concentrated? When costs and benefits are concentrated, the policy is determined by a clash between interest groups. When profits are concentrated and costs are diffused, the policy is called clientelist: the public authorities grant the lobbies what they ask for. When costs are concentrated and benefits diffuse, the policy is entrepreneurial. A moral entrepreneur (Becker, 1995) seizes a subject and urges the government to take action that entails costs for certain interest groups. When costs and benefits are diffuse, the policy is called majoritarian. Majority and entrepreneurial policies inevitably take place within public debate. Interest groups and clientelist policies can take place behind the scenes. Interest groups, often represented by a meta-organization, are involved in clientelist policies (obtaining subsidies, tariffs, tax benefits, etc.), in interest groups policies (restrictions on imports, putting in place regulations that favor one group over another), and in entrepreneurial policies (protecting a sector against political entrepreneurs, such as the meat industry in the face of attempts to reduce consumption). Evaluating the possible weight of the interest groups, the influence of the meta-organizations representing the various industrial sectors, thus assumes identifying the political situation in which they are involved.

CONCLUSION

In a democratic society, even Rousseau and Madison who are extremely suspicious of intermediary bodies believe they are inevitable and a part of the game of democracy. In particular, they have a fundamental role of representation:

> First and foremost, interest groups *represent* their constituents before government. They are a primary link between citizens and their government, forming a channel of access through which members voice their opinions to those who govern them. The democratic process can be described in the most eloquent language and be based on the noblest intentions, but in the real world of politics it must provide some means by which manufacturers, environmentalists, conservative Christians, construction workers, or whoever can speak to government about their specific policy preferences and have the government listen. For many people, interest groups are the most important mechanism by which their views are represented before the three branches of government. (Berry & Wilcox, 2018, p. 7; original emphasis)

They also have other roles such as agenda-setting or changing perceptions of the environment with respect to a sector. The democratic principle presupposes the peaceful confrontation of political opinions and a majority decision, respecting the rights of the minority. Interest groups help frame opinions and thus clarify the multiple perspectives according to which a political issue can be approached.

Politically, and in terms of general economic well-being, business meta-organizations can have both negative and positive effects. It is possible to synthesize these effects as shown in Table 3.1 (see below).

Two questions arise on the theoretical level. The first is to ask whether business meta-organizations in a country (or at the global level) are effective or not, especially if they have a concrete impact on decisions made at the political level. Indeed, research has shown that fragmentation, diversity, and under-resourcing can make these organizations very ineffective (Bennett, 1998; Grant, 1987; Lanzalaco, 1992). Lynn and McKeown (1988) have shown, for example, that American business meta-organizations in the 1980s were more fragmented and therefore probably less effective than Japanese business meta-organizations, which were organized in a more hierarchical and coordinated fashion (grouped, for example, in the same building). Laumann and Knoke (1987, 1988) have shown that public action can be broken down

Table 3.1   *Potential (negative and positive) effects of firms' collective action devices*

Potential Negative Effects of Business Meta-organizations	Potential Positive Effects of Business Meta-organizations
To orient the political agenda towards the topics that interest them, and that are not the most important topics for the community	To improve the quality of public decision-making by reducing search and consensus costs
To obtain political decisions in their favor (tax provisions, tariff provisions, subsidies, technical decisions) to the detriment of collective well-being	To improve regulation by reducing monitoring costs once the decision is made
To block political decisions that are in the sense of collective well-being but against the interests that they defend	To improve collective answers to regulative evolutions
To block innovations that threaten their interests	To accelerate some necessary adaptations through services to their members
To delay the necessary adaptations of society and the economy	

into relatively isolated areas and that, in the context of these isolated areas, interest groups often represented by business meta-organizations could structurally guide the public decision in the direction of their interest. Aldrich (2018) believes that American society is moving towards a weakening of the elite cohesion, a fragmentation, and that in this context trade associations and business meta-organizations can have a negative effect.

The second theoretical question is to ask oneself whether, assuming that these business meta-organizations do have an impact on political decisions, this impact is positive (contributing to a good growth dynamic) or whether it is negative (poor allocation of resources and slower growth). Business meta-organizations, like Janus, have two faces: they can be detrimental to society or contribute to the resolution of contemporary societal problems (Marques, 2017).

Unfortunately, the answers to these two questions are difficult to establish. They involve the mobilization of multiple methodologies, operating at multiple levels, and combining quantitative and qualitative approaches, which is rarely the case.

CHAPTER SUMMARY

For the theorists of modern democracy, such as Rousseau and the American and French revolutionaries of the late eighteenth century, organized groups (which they call "factions") are dangerous in that they can distort the democratic game. Therefore, for example, the legislation put in place by the French Revolution prohibited firms from organizing collectively.

As an economist, Mancur Olson argued that organized interest groups were diverting resources for the pursuit of political rent, undermined the optimal allocation of resources in the economy, and had a dynamic negative effect on the economy, innovation, and growth.

On the other hand, other approaches show that, at the political level, interest groups play a vital role in producing information relevant to political decision-making, and that governments, deprived of this information, would be partly blind and could make bad decisions. And, economically, studies show that business meta-organizations can foster innovation (by helping standardization, by taking part in the resolution of collective problems, by the sharing of good practices).

In practice, the analysis is complicated. The world of politico-economic decision-making is indeed balkanized: it operates by subdomains, which should all be studied in and of themselves.

The debate remains open, knowing that the two opposing theses are true without knowing exactly in what proportion; that is to say, without being able to say whether, globally, the economic and political effects of business meta-organizations are positive or negative.

NOTES

1. Our translation from the French: "L'intérêt personnel n'est point à craindre; il est isolé, chacun a le sien; la grande difficulté vient de l'intérêt par lequel un citoyen s'accorde avec quelques autres seulement. Celui-ci permet de se concerter, de se liguer. Par lui se combinent les projets dangereux pour la communauté, par lui se forment les ennemis publics les plus redoutables. Qu'on ne soit donc pas étonné si l'ordre social exige avec tant de vigueur de ne point laisser les simples citoyens disposer de corporations."

2. Our translation from the French: "Il doit sans doute être permis à tous les citoyens de s'assembler; mais il ne doit pas être permis aux citoyens de certaines professions de s'assembler pour leurs prétendus intérêts communs; il n'y a plus de corporation dans l'État; il n'y a plus que l'intérêt particulier de chaque individu, et l'intérêt général. Il n'est permis à personne d'inspirer aux citoyens un intérêt intermédiaire, de les séparer de la chose publique par un esprit de corporation" ("Bulletin de l'Assemblée Nationale du 14 juin 1791," *Gazette nationale ou le moniteur universel*, 15 juin 1791 – Deuxième année de la Liberté, dans *Réimpression de l'Ancien Moniteur*, Volume 8, p. 661).

3. Our translation from the French: "Nulle société, club, association de citoyens ne peuvent avoir sous aucune forme une existence politique, ni exercer aucune action ni inspection sur les actes des pouvoirs constitués et des autorités légales; ... sous aucun prétexte, ils ne pourront paraître sous un nom collectif ... pour former des pétitions ou des deputations" (Décret du 29 septembre 1791, préambule, *Archives Parlementaires*; 1ères series, Volume 29, p. 624).

4. French revolutionaries like Le Chapelier explicitly refer to Rousseau in their speeches. Madison had also read Rousseau carefully (Conniff, 1975).
5. "Il importe donc, pour avoir bien l'énoncé de la volonté générale, qu'il n'y ait pas de société partielle dans l'État, et que chaque citoyen n'opine que d'après lui ... Que s'il y a des sociétés partielles, il en faut multiplier le nombre et en prévenir l'inégalité ... Ces précautions sont les seules bonnes pour que la volonté générale soit toujours éclairée et que le peuple ne se trompe point."
6. Even if the establishment of a business meta-organization in the District of Columbia is not a reliable indicator, it constitutes a reasonable index of the search for political influence.

PART II

Within trade associations and other meta-organizations

4. Firms' collective action devices as a mix of heterarchy and hierarchy

The organizations we see around us (firms, hospitals, schools, administrations, etc.) have characteristic features that are familiar to us. Their members are individuals. They are paid by the organization for the work they do and carry out this work in functional departments or business units of the organization whose borders are often quite well defined. If they leave the organization, they are fairly easily replaced (even in the case of the chief executive officer [CEO] or of an expert in a specialty) to the extent that there is a labor market that allows the recruitment of new members. Each individual is part of a hierarchical line that structures the organization – work is divided and coordinated under the responsibility of superiors. These individuals work for the organization; the organization does not work for them (the company, for example, works for its shareholders by satisfying the demands of its customers). The theory of organizations has developed by studying mainly this type of organization, which can be defined as follows: "clear departmental boundaries, clear lines of authority, detailed reporting mechanisms, and formal decision making procedures" (Powell, 1990, p. 303).

Firms' collective action devices (FCADs) are organizations of a different nature and have many peculiarities. Their members are organizations, not individuals. They are the ones who finance the organization, not the other way around. As a result, the more members of the organization, the higher the income – the reverse of what happens traditionally. The organization works for its members, not the other way around, and is highly dependent on them; they can easily cease to be members and no longer contribute. There is no explicit hierarchy between the members – all are on an equal footing (of *relative* equality, as will be seen). Members are constantly negotiating and voting on the decisions to be made. If they do not agree, they take to the floor to say so (voice), they can often block the decision (right of veto), and, if the conflict is deep, they can easily leave the organization (exit), which makes them realize a direct economy since they have more fees to settle. The differences between traditional organizations and FCADs are illustrated in Table 4.1 (see below).

The hierarchy of the traditional organization is today being challenged. The idea of freedom-based companies, holacracy, and so on, is spreading. At the same time, heterarchy as an organizational principle coexists with hierarchy.

Table 4.1   *Traditional organization versus meta-organization*

	Traditional Organization	Meta-organization
Aims of the organization	Products, services	Collectively control external organizations influencing the surrounding environment
Members	Individuals, paid by the organization and inserted in a hierarchy	Organizations financing the global organization with their contributions, operating in an egalitarian way
Inner organization	Business units	Committees
Mode of appointment of department heads	Appointed head of departments	Elected (chairperson of a committee)
Decision-making process	Hierarchical	By consensus and by vote

Our study supports this idea, since in meta-organizations two sub-organizations cohabit, with staff organized according to a hierarchical principle, and the members making decisions according to a heterarchic principle. How do these two logics combine in practice in a meta-organization?

THE NOTION OF HETERARCHY

To analyze societies or non-hierarchical organizations, we can speak of a "meshwork" (De Landa, 1997) or of a "panarchy" (Gunderson & Holling, 2001), portraying the idea of a total sharing of power between the members of the organization or firm. Max Weber already opposed bureaucracy and collegiality (Waters, 1989). The most commonly used notion, however, is that of heterarchy (Stark, 2009) as opposed to hierarchy. It may be applied to very different contexts (neuroscience, for example, has shown that brain function is often non-hierarchical), including organizational. The most commonly used definition is from anthropology:

> The relation of elements to one another when they are unranked, or when they possess the potential for being ranked in a number of different ways, depending on systemic requirements. (Crumley, 1979, p. 144)

Kontopoulos, a social scientist (1993, p. 381) provides another: "a partially ordered level structure implicating a rampant interactional complexity." The important thing here is that the relations between heterarchy and hierarchy are complex and intertwined ("a partially ordered level structure" suggests that there may be an element of hierarchy in heterarchy – we will come back to this later).

In addition, Girard and Stark (2003, p. 87) describe three fundamental characteristics for a heterarchical organization: relations of interdependence with considerable heterogeneity and limited hierarchy. We find here the idea that the heterarchy combines in practice with elements, even limited, of hierarchy, but emphasizes the interdependence between highly heterogeneous actors. These actors are often themselves organizations. Their heterogeneity may derive from their size and their resources, but also from their status: firms, states, non-governmental organizations (NGOs), in the case, for example, of multistakeholder organizations. This heterogeneity produces a cognitive effect specific to heterarchies, underlined by Girard and Stark (2002) who speak of "distributed intelligence." This distributed intelligence is favored by information technologies (Ronfeldt, 1996). It can take the form of coopetition (Brandenburger & Nalebuff, 1996; Yami et al., 2010):

> [Heterarchies] are highly cooperative as well as highly competitive governing regimes. (Reihlen & Mone, 2012, p. 113)

Mayntz does not use the term heterarchy, but by analyzing the functioning of the interorganizational networks, she defines the characteristics by specifying certain elements:

> Where interorganizational networks are able to produce
> * collective outputs intentionally,
> * through interaction, and
> * in spite of diverging interests of their members,
> their dominant logic might most fittingly be described as negotiation. (Mayntz, 1993, p. 14)

We see here the heterogeneity of the actors (diverging interests), but Mayntz introduces the notion of collective intention, which explains in particular the interdependence between the heterogeneous actors; interdependence that is realized in the form of interactions whose dominant logic is the negotiation.

What organizational forms can heterarchy take? Jessop (1998) sees three possibilities. The first is interpersonal networking. The idea is close to the notion advanced by Galambos (1966) of the dinner club association. The second is the creation of a true organization that pursues common objectives even if the interests are heterogeneous – "a self-organization of inter-organizational relations" (one could speak of a meta-organization). Inspired by Luhmann (1992), Jessop sees a possible third level: intersystemic steering:

> This form of governance involves the coordination of differentiated institutional orders or functional systems (such as the economic, political, legal, scientific, or educational systems), each of which has its own complex operational logic such that

it is impossible to exercise effective overall control of its development from outside that system. (Jessop, 1998, p. 33)

Table 4.2   Hierarchy versus heterarchy

	Hierarchy	Heterarchy
Advantages	Clear decision-making chain	Good-quality information
	Responds well to fast-developing crises	Fair decisions reflect popular consensus
	Rules and responsibilities known to all	Contributions of disparate segments
	Political interactions few and formalized	valued
	Political maintenance of the system is	Variety of solutions to problems
	low	presented
	Powerful means of security	
	Defends the organization	
	Suppresses internal dissent	
Disadvantages	Slow movement of information to the	Consensus is slow
	top, especially true of subversive activity	Dialogue requires constant maintenance
	Formal and elaborate internal security	Cacophonous voices and choices
	Expedient decisions not necessarily	
	popular	
	High popular dissatisfaction	
	Considerable investment in coercion	
	High security costs	

Source: Based on Crumley (2005, p. 43).

We can now summarize the differences between hierarchy and heterarchy in Table 4.2 (see above). From all these elements, we can specify the notion of heterarchy. One can speak of heterarchy when heterogeneous actors, with divergent interests, are aware of their interdependence and define a common goal, which they pursue by setting up a form of organization, refusing the principle of a formal and justified hierarchy, based on negotiation aimed at building consensus or compromise. It should be noted that heterarchy in practice combines with hierarchy (Crumley, 1995) and that these modes of combination must be studied.

THE CONSTITUTIONAL ISSUE IN A HETERARCHY

The clue to the heterarchical dimension in FCADs is the language that refers not to the traditional organization and its hierarchical structure, but to phenomena related to internal governance. Von Schnurbein (2009) highlights patterns of governance in trade associations and unions. With regard to trade associations, he distinguishes between "delegate governance," more egalitarian between members, and "inner-circle governance," where the real influence comes from a few big companies that dominate the market (von Schnurbein, 2009, p. 109). The governance of the meta-organization is seen by actors through the lens of political metaphors. In our interviews (see methodological appendix), words appeared that related to political language: "elections," "federative form," "political cooking," "representativeness without parties," "undemocratic," "managed democracy." The question of the constitution, in the political sense, of the organization was often mentioned by the actors. This has arisen since this type of organization existed:

> When associations are first being formed, however, and at other critical times, there may be misgivings in some quarters about the consequences of membership. Small firms ask whether the association will be dominated by a few big firms; and large ones do not want to be overruled by a great number of small firms with a low proportion of total output. These and other doubts and suspicions, if they occur, will have to be met in some way. A carefully balanced constitution will often help to do this. (McRobie et al., 1957, p. 177)

In a meta-organization, imbalances result from the heterogeneity of the members. The constitution helps to build trust, attract new members, and channel conflict. Discussions on constitutional rules arise at the moment of the creation of the organization, but also throughout its existence:

> Negotiation in interorganizational networks is not only about single issues such as a specific policy decision, a joint research project, etc.; it is also, and often more importantly, about the institutional arrangement itself – the constitution, as it were, of a given sector of society. (Mayntz, 1993, p. 17)

The constitution of the meta-organization is regularly "renegotiated" as the meta-organization and the evolution of its activity grow. It provides the general framework for collective action:

> [Business meta-organizations] commonly have a constitution, which sets forth in highly general terms the purposes of the association, defines membership or classes of members, and authorizes governance by a governing board and a set of officers. The bylaws are generally unremarkable specifications of membership classes, officers, their duties, and their selection process, annual meetings, standing committees, and the like. (Lynn & McKeown, 1988, pp. 55–6)

This "meta-organizational constitution" makes it possible to describe the organization as a "decided order" (Ahrne and Brunsson, 2011), and one can find in the constitution elements on membership, rules, as well as on monitoring and sanctions.

The first constitution of the trade association we studied was that of an egalitarian democracy: each of the six founding firms paid the same contribution and each had one vote. In reality, there was no vote and the meta-organization worked with consensus, which is never easy but still easier when there are only six people around the table. With the scaling phase, things changed. On the one hand, large firms joined the trade association. It was decided that contributions would be larger for these large firms than for small ones. On the other hand, the number of members greatly increased. Soon, tensions appeared and it was necessary to pose the constitutional problem once more. This is consistent with Coleman (1985), who stated that the more associations become involved in policy participation activities, the more tensions they will feel internally as organizations. It was necessary to manage both the temptations for certain sub-sectors to become autonomous and the tensions between large and small firms.

To constitutionally manage the first problem, it was the form of the federation between subsectors that served as a reference:

> As soon as it started to work, there were centrifugal forces. Wind, solar photo-voltaic, solar water heater, everyone wanted his own "shop." I managed to bring everyone back into the association by opting for a federative form.

The president wanted to convey the message that in a federation, each state retains its autonomy. It was necessary to determine the operating rules of this federation to manage the tensions between large and small firms. There, the political reference was the regime of consensus democracy:

> The president [of the trade association] is elected by direct universal suffrage. When we started to grow, we asked the big companies to pay a little more and we gave them more votes. It is a bit of political cooking; we took care that the big ones cannot impose their points of view. In any case, they often hated each other [mention is made of two large firms directly competing with each other].

One of the obsessions in the constitution of the organization is representative-ness. As the exit costs of the organization are low, the possibility of creating a competing trade association is constant, ensuring that all components of the "sector" feel represented. Committees, in addition to their technical function of defending the interests of a particular subsector or dealing with a cross-cutting problem, also have this function:[1]

> We seek balanced representation of the subsectors and we want to avoid over-representation.

If, for example, some actors did not feel well represented on the board or on the committees, they might be tempted to create their own trade association. The search for balance is very delicate and uncertain: the elective process can lead to crisis situations. If, at the end of the votes, the big companies that contribute most financially to the organization do not have some key positions, and if, after the same vote, the small companies do not feel represented or if they have the impression that the big companies have monopolized all the key positions and seized the power, the organization risks breaking down. Since, by definition, the vote is uncertain, all work is done before the vote, and subtle calculations are made to anticipate the result:

> We have electoral colleges. A large company has a larger contribution. We did the math: our small colleges exceed the voting weight of big firms. We wondered if the big guys could agree to get one of their representatives elected. In fact, candidates from large companies have not been elected.

In this election, the candidates supported by large companies were known. The voting rights being proportional to the subscription, the risk was high that these candidates were all elected and that the big firms seized power over the meta-organization. It would therefore have been managed only in the interest of large firms and not in the interest of the industry as a whole (which is often the case, as Barnett's 2013 study has shown). For the durability of the trade association and its good functioning, it was hoped that this was not to be the case.

In reality, in these heterarchical organizations, one is constantly seeking complex balance and the constitution is created to try to ensure this. Since there is no explicit hierarchy, everyone must have the floor, decisions must be made respecting these different voices. At the same time, it is clear that some actors have more weight than others. As the functioning of heterarchy can be easily blocked either because some voices are missing from the consensus, or because the participants in the heterarchy can decide to leave, it is necessary to find a constitution that expresses the myth of equality and assures representativeness of all, while considering differences of power. If the big monopolize the power, the small leave (in many sectors one finds two trade associations, one representing the big firms and the other the small ones). If big firms feel that, although they provide a substantial share of the organization's budget, they are dominated by small firms in great number, they may threaten to leave. The constitution must assure everyone that their voice is heard, and that no one will exit because of the ease of exit:

> If a decision is not favorable to you, you have the choice between leaving the association or accepting the governance, the decision. Leaving is very easy.

One therefore finds constitutively the categories put forward by Hirschman in his 1970 treatise: exit, voice, and loyalty.

How, in practice, does one try to frame the elective process so that it can produce the desired balance of representativity that is inherently uncertain? First, by shifting the different elections in time:

> The members of the board are elected and then only the chairpersons of the committees.

Once the results of the vote on the board are known, one knows who is represented, and in what way. So, one also knows who is not. When members vote for the chairs of the committees, the board tries to find a global balance of representativeness, to which all members agree because it is in their own interest, no matter their size or special feature:

> [The trade association] is very much about respect for governance and the members understand it. This is the key to our efficiency. The big firms know that it is not in their interest to crush SMEs [small and medium-sized enterprises].

By definition, a heterarchy is a mode of organization that is based on the rejection of the hierarchy. But heterarchies bring together very heterogeneous actors, and dissymmetrical relationships exist between these actors, engendering power relations, real or potential. As exit of the heterarchy is easy, the work of constitutional elaboration (that Mayntz rightly points out is constantly itself subject to bitter negotiations, is never settled once and for all) is crucial and difficult. It will consist in making everyone feel represented in the decision-making process, while taking into account the dissymmetries existing between the heterogeneous actors. In practice, the functioning is that of a "managed democracy," according to the expression of an actor we interviewed. How, in practice, do actors live the functioning of heterarchy?

THE EXPERIENCE OF A HETERARCHY

Ahrne and Brunsson (2008) describe meta-organizations as "boring" organizations. During the interviews we conducted, an interlocutor referred to a trade association that had existed for decades, managed by two people in a small Paris apartment. This association assumed the routine tasks of this type of organization: collect the (small) fees of members, collect data, write a newsletter, organize a meeting from time to time. Many meta-organizations are in this quasi-dormant situation and can rightly be described as boring organizations. On the other hand, when they are engaged in important negotiations with the state, the situation is very different. Here heterarchy is active; the experience is then very different from boredom. During an interview, we asked one of the presidents of the trade association we studied to describe how he perceived his work. He laughed first. Then there was a silence, and finally this sentence: "It's very complicated." Several interlocutors, having often worked in other types of organizations, highlighted the deeply conflicting nature of heterarchy:

> I discovered the violence of these internal conflicts.
> The big shock is to experience the conflicts between companies.

Between the dormant meta-organization and the active meta-organization, the difference lies in the stakes of collective action. If these stakes are high, the tensions are immediately very strong:

> They all eat from the same bowl.
> Centrifugal tendencies were still there.

These tensions have an interpersonal dimension that appears in the interviews we conducted:

> Very strong egos.
> Among them, things were often getting heated.
> They hated each other physically.

It is the president of the meta-organization who is at the center of these conflicts of ego:

> As president, the most unpleasant situation is conflict.

Insofar as it is he who leads the negotiations with the public authorities, he finds himself caught between the hammer and the anvil, between the public authorities and the members of the meta-organization:

> I happened to be rapped on the knuckles by a some of my troops who reproached me for having capitulated.
> They thought I was too lukewarm.

These interpersonal tensions express or combine with the tensions between firms that form the sector. For example, distributors, installers, and producers have radically different positions on trade policies. Installers and distributors favor cheap imports while producers want to block them. A united position with regard to the public authorities is then difficult to establish and collective action can be paralyzed:

> For example, if we favor the French industry on photovoltaics, we will have higher prices than if we buy Chinese, which is the wish of developers.

But, in just about every FCAD, tensions are high between small and large firms. The large ones provide a large share of the contributions and therefore of the organization's budget. They seek to impose their views by playing on the possibility of their exit from the organization, while knowing not to go too far as collective action remains important for them (Barnett, 2018):

> Blackmail over exit – it happens. It comes mostly from big companies. But we know they have no interest in leaving us. You know, it's a bit of a poker game. They can see the minister, and they do not hesitate to do so, but their lobbying is more effective if it is relayed through the trade association.

For their part, small businesses feel dominated and are, as one actor says, "skinned alive." They often feel they are not listened to:

> In the trade association, it is good that there are small firms, they justify it being a generalist trade association, but they have no voice.
> We were asked our opinion but it was useless.

They feel that they must adhere to decisions made by big firms in the latter's interest and "swallow bitter pills." The intensity of conflict is one of the characteristics of heterarchical functioning. It makes its weakness, but also its wealth:

> It is difficult to obtain unanimity. It has the merit of putting on the table proposals that are discussed.

Conflicts highlight a plurality of visions and solutions and measure the political weight of these visions and solutions within the meta-organization. The distributed intelligence attributed to heterarchies by Girard and Stark (2003) comes from, and is expressed by, the perpetual conflicts between heterogeneous members of the organization. These conflicts can be resolved if the members of the organization believe that the benefits of collective action outweigh the costs. This is possible when members of the collective action mechanism recognize that the device produces results that benefit them:

> We arrived at compromises, consensus. Many thanks [to the president], because he was strong and because he brought back results.

How are these compromises obtained? A negative condition is the delimitation of negotiating corridors:

> [The] individual interests define a limited corridor (or window) of possible agreement. (Mayntz, 1993, p. 14)

It is agreed that certain directly conflicting issues between members or those directly conflicting with the interests of other groups must be avoided (Laumann & Knoke, 1988, p. 22). In our case, that of renewable energies in France, a near-consensus emerged to avoid addressing the nuclear issue. France having opted for massive electricity production via the nuclear sector, two options were available for renewable energies: either to present themselves as an alternative solution to nuclear power, or to try to develop without calling into question the nuclear power option. It is this second option that was chosen. Heterarchies are inherently conflictual. They can succeed in negotiating compromises and consensus by deciding to exclude from the field of discussion the most sensitive topics to focus on those about which agreement is possible. When the 13 American colonies decided to build a federal state after declaring their independence, for example, the issue of slavery was removed from the discussions and was a taboo subject (Ellis, 2000). In heterarchies, the definition of a corridor of possible agreement is probably decisive for allowing heterarchy to work. Methodologically, it is therefore interesting when one studies a meta-organization to ask on which topics there is a consensus not to address them. Once this negative condition is met, it is about building a certain community of views, which is always fragile. This is the work that is done by the organization, that is, the president, the delegate general, and the staff:

> In 80 percent of cases, we have a common position.
> It takes a community of views. It is not very serious that there are different opinions.
> We come to build consensus, intermediate positions.

The organization must succeed in maintaining the Jeffersonian principle: "every difference of opinion is not a difference of principle." Even if they feel that they have had to admit a decision that favors other actors more than them, that they have not been listened to, the actors recognize that a collective good has been obtained, which would not have been obtained individually. In this mode of conflict resolution, heterarchy manages to overcome the tensions within which it operates. But the process is experienced by the actors as frustrating, wearying. More than boredom, it is fatigue and frustration that mark the experience in this type of organization. In the same interview, an actor expressed it as follows:

> We repeat ourselves a lot. It uses a lot of energy. We wear ourselves out. It was a little tiring, these ego stories.

The president of a company participating in the meetings of a multistakeholder meta-organization whose members are very heterogeneous analyzes his dual experience of both the interest and frustration of these permanent and often interminable negotiations:

> An interesting thing and at the same time a frustrating thing. In the United Nations stuff, we spend a lot of time to get things moving by just one centimeter. We need people who manage this international time ... This type of organization always goes at the pace of the slowest.

If the meta-organization fails to build consensus in the compromise, if the differences of opinion appear as divergent principles, then the conflict results in a split:

> There are schisms. It's a story of divisions and merging again (but it's rare that it merges again). The small actors are skinned alive. There are many trade associations born by split.

That is what happened in our case study. In France, there was a trade association representing the wind energy sector, France Énergie Éolienne (FEE) and a trade association representing all renewable energies (SER – Syndicat des Énergies Renouvelables). Both were trying to obtain a favorable policy from the government. The government received them both and played the division. A merger was realized, FEE integrating with SER, becoming its branch for wind energy while continuing to exist. We have seen that the constitution that was adopted was of the federal form, that is to say, guaranteeing the maintenance of a certain autonomy for its members. Nevertheless, in a federation, a secession can intervene. And that is what happened. Internal conflicts quickly escalated. A constitutional amendment solution of heterarchy was sought, but without success:

> We tried to amend the marriage contract but didn't find a solution.

FEE then decided to leave SER. On the one hand, it considered that the resources that it contributed to the SER through contributions from its members were not only for wind power but were also used for other purposes. On the other hand, it felt that it had lost its freedom of speech with regard to the government. Finally, as always, conflicts of vision were coupled with conflicts of persons. Jefferson's principle then, opposed to Caesar's:

> The opposite version of the union is strength. There are always some who prefer to be the king in their village than the second in the city.[2]

Although members are organizations, the experience of a meta-organization is far from being decoupled from human and personal considerations. The experience of a heterarchy is therefore composed of permanent threats to departure, and the risk of competing organizations being formed. This is how many trade associations were created from a split with an earlier trade association. Meta-organizations thus tend to proliferate.

THE HETERARCHY/HIERARCHY COMBINATION

Theorists of heterarchy have noted that there is no pure heterarchic form (as there is probably no pure hierarchical form; March, 1962) and that, in practice, heterarchy and hierarchy combine. How remains to be understood. As we have seen, organizations of a purely heterarchical nature appeared in the eighteenth and nineteenth centuries in the form of what Galambos (1966) called the dinner club associations. Business leaders found themselves in a place at a certain time, usually outside work hours, often for dinner, and talked about problems common to their sector. The organizational dimension was reduced to a minimum; it was sufficient to fix the place and time of the meeting. These dinner club associations turned into organizations in the late nineteenth and early twentieth centuries that hired staff. We can then speak of meta-organizations; organizations whose members are organizations but which themselves exist as organizations. In these organizations, we can distinguish two entities: one heterarchical and the other hierarchical. The hierarchy is there to ensure the organizational functioning of the heterarchy, it plays a supporting role, is not very visible, and remains minimal – hence the notion of minimalist organization (Halliday, Powell & Granfors, 1987). But things are actually more complex.

A heterarchy arises when heterogeneous actors decide to pursue a common goal by refusing a hierarchical order. No actor can therefore directly and legitimately impose their power on another. But, that does not mean that there are no power relations within heterarchy. In reality, two phenomena are at play. On the one hand, the actors recognize a relationship of interdependence between them, knowing that the possibility of breaking out of heterarchy, of secession, exists permanently. The most powerful actors are self-limiting in the exercise of their power. This is the case for large firms in trade associations. They contribute the most to the budget, often have voting rights superior to small firms, but know that it is preferable, due to their institutional environment (state, NGOs), to present a united front. On the other hand, as noted by Crumley (1979), heterarchy does not, in practice, mean perfect equality between the actors but rather a multiplicity of different hierarchical orders, one of which does not obviously prevail over the other. In our case, six small companies founded the trade association. Large companies only joined the meta-organization much later. The entry of these big companies led to a change of constitution, profoundly changed the functioning of the trade association and they quickly occupied positions of power. But, for a long time, the small founding companies kept some influence and positions of power (board of directors, chairing committees) that were not related to their size but with the prestige and esteem related to their status as founding members (what the Romans called *auctoritas*; Arendt, 1961). This period ended when one of the founding members, traditionally re-elected as chair of the committee representing his subsector, was no longer re-elected as the large companies decided to take control of this committee. On the other hand, heterarchy functions at the level of the meta-organization with a hierarchical rule:

> There is a single trade association, which speaks on behalf of everyone, but within the trade association there are committees. The committees do not speak directly to political actors and administration.

The committees therefore submit hierarchically to the governing bodies of the meta-organization. We are not far away from democratic centralism as theoretically defined by Lenin (the practical application of which was made subject to debate): "freedom of discussion, unity of action."[3] The trade association version looks like this:

> It chatters, it chatters and then in the end we see things emerge. The committees decide what actions to take.

But then, once a consensus is reached at the committee level, the president of the union implements the decision and negotiates, for example, with the public authorities:

> The negotiations with the public authorities, it is the president.

There is therefore a hierarchical-type rule in the very functioning of heterarchy, discussions with the public authorities are the preserve of the president. In that sense, trade associations resemble bureaucracies with a hierarchy of authority, norms for conducting internal and external relations, and a set of formal principles for distinguishing between members and non-members (Staber, 1987). Moreover, as we have seen, historically, dinner club associations were transformed into meta-organizations when they hired permanent staff. If meta-organizations grow in size, a classic organizational part is created in the form of a hierarchy. In our case, a permanent member of staff of the organization analyzes the process, as follows:

> At first, everyone knows everyone. In the end, yes, some misunderstandings appeared. People discovered that there was a committee session they would like to attend. Yes. That's why the trade association must organize itself, be more rigorous

about everything, manage information. In my time, there was very little hierarchy. Now, there must be a general secretary and deputy general secretaries. We create hierarchy again. It's an interesting phenomenon. It's a bit true of any organization.

Staff are gradually being hired to provide secretarial services for the committees and, most importantly, for the organization to respond to requests from member companies:

> You have to answer, including trivia, very small problems. To retain them [firms' members], you have to be responsive, listening.

The principle is that each company has an interlocutor whom they can contact. For those who participate in the work of a committee, it is the permanent staff who provide the secretariat. Small committees share a permanent member of staff. They are the correspondents of the firms. This dimension is very important because companies, if they perceive that the trade association does not respond to their individual demands, can cease to be members and choose to exit. Of course, the hierarchical part of the organization will examine the issues, collect and process the information, format and analyze it in order to prepare the communication and the negotiations with the public authorities and, more generally, with the environment of the sector. But it is at the level of the relationship between the president and the managing director that the central relationship between heterarchy and hierarchy takes place. A general secretary describes it as well:

> The kingpin, the president and general secretary, is central. The president is an officer of the Legion of Honor and can try to call a minister; the secretary is the technician that we do not see.

Obviously, the rise of the staff, the hierarchical part of the organization, is experienced by some members, often small businesses, as a drift of the organization:

> As often, that's one of the problems; they became permanent organizations. There were permanent staff. They had escaped from the members. They were communicating for their egos.

In addition, there is a turnover problem. In contact with member companies, permanent employees may be tempted to leave the meta-organization to enter one of these companies:

> We had trouble keeping the staff; they were hunted by members.

At the top of the hierarchical part of the organization is a general secretary, general manager, or managing director. His or her role is essential for the proper functioning of the organization. Naylor, who served in this position, analyzed its importance and role in the 1920s:

> [W]e must admit that since the business of being secretary now calls for special training it is becoming more and more of a profession. (Naylor, 1921, p. 208)

In 1920, the American Society of Association Executives (ASAE) was created. Its European equivalent, the European Society of Association Executives (ESAE), based in Zurich, was created in 1979. Naylor analyzes the role of the secretary or managing director around a few characteristics. The members of the organization generally want it to be discreet and efficient:

> He says little and thinks much. (Naylor, 1921, p. 215)

In our case study, the managing director attends board meetings, but he is actually silent. He only speaks if asked a question. The secretary must also be completely "impartial in his relations with all members of the association" (Naylor, 1921, p. 210). This impartiality is also expressed in their role as a "blue helmet" (like a member of the United Nations peacekeeping force). He or she must, as far as possible, try to defuse the conflicts between members:

> One of the most important duties of a secretary – constituting, one might say about three-quarters of his value – is that of keeping the members all feeling right towards one another. (Naylor, 1921, p. 220)

In particular, he or she must strive to resolve the conflicts between people that come to aggravate conflicts of interest between firms:

> Rumor, gossip, and misinformation generally play a large part in stirring up ill feeling among members which may lead to disastrous results. It must be the secretary's duty to kill the trouble at the start, to forestall the destructive tendencies by quietly and effectively instilling the disposition for harmony in the mind of each member. The secretary should be a constant harbinger of truth. (Naylor, 1921, p. 221)

The meta-organization can thus be represented as a combination of heterarchy and hierarchy as shown in Figure 4.1.

The link between the heterarchic part and the hierarchical part of the meta-organization operates in practice thanks to the double kingpins, the president and general secretary or managing director. During one of our interviews, a president expresses this connection with the words "Me and my staff." Relations between the president and the managing director or general

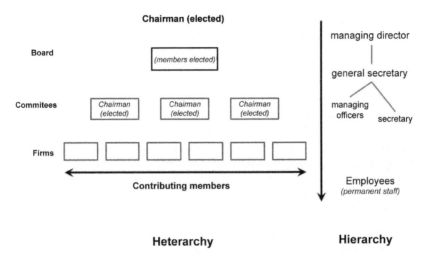

Figure 4.1   *Meta-organization as heterarchy and hierarchy*

secretary depend on the status of the president. In some meta-organizations, the president does not exercise his or her function full-time. He or she remains an employee of her company. In others, he or she is a salaried employee of the meta-organization, which potentially gives him or her greater independence. In our case study, the two systems succeeded one another. At first, the president continued to be an employee of his company; today, he is an employee of the trade association. It may be noted that if the hierarchical part develops, it can become autonomous with respect to the heterarchical part and acquire a power related to the information and the knowledge it has:

> [T]he secretariat has a greater knowledge than members of where issues are and what forces are at work, as they are dealing with these issues full time, whereas members are only periodically involved. This difference in knowledge and perception can cause tensions between the secretariat and the members. (Boleat, 1996, p. 108)

CONCLUSION

This chapter has analyzed the inner functioning of FCADs as the combination of two organizational dimensions: heterarchy and hierarchy. Business meta-organizations are based initially on rejection of the hierarchical relation, which tries to express their constitution. This is expressed by permanent internal negotiations, which can sometimes show the existence of tensions between members, thus raising the question of the compatibility of these two logics within the same organizational device. Nevertheless, in practice, they seek to combine the advantages of heterarchy (freedom of expression, diversity of points of view, creativity of solutions) with those of hierarchy (mobilization of expertise, continuity of this expertise, efficiency in action). The balance is always fragile and must be renegotiated constantly, because of the permanent threat of conflict.

We must now perform a dynamic analysis of FCADs in the next chapter and study the way in which this type of organization is born and developed. Some of the points that have been mentioned will be found in the analysis, such as the conflict dimension and the threat of an exit by the members of the organization, individually or collectively by creating a new meta-organization.

CHAPTER SUMMARY

FCADs as meta-organizations are organizations of a particular type. The hierarchical principle, if present, is not central. We can then speak of heterarchy, and, in practice, of a combination of hierarchy and heterarchy.

One can speak of heterarchy when heterogeneous actors, with divergent interests, are aware of their interdependence and define a common goal, which they pursue by setting up a form of organization rejecting the principle of a formal hierarchy and being based on negotiation aimed at building consensus or compromise. Ahrne and Brunsson (2008) described these organizations as boring. Boring undoubtedly characterizes these organizations when they are dormant. When they are active, the actors experience them as highly conflictual, with the permanent threat of exit from members, and in constant search for compromise and consensus, making them organizations that are both exhausting and frustrating. For them to work, they must respect Jefferson's principle ("every difference of opinion is not a difference of principle"). But they are permanently threatened by the principle of Caesar ("I would rather be first in a village than second in Rome"). The conflict can indeed lead to a split of the meta-organization, with the creation of a smaller one.

In practice, heterarchy and hierarchy (in particular, the permanent staff of the meta-organization) combine and articulate. The keystones of the operation are the double kingpins, the president (elected) and managing director or general secretary.

NOTES

1.   Some business meta-organizations are tempted, for this reason, to multiply the number of committees and the number of members in each committee:

Many trade associations have governing bodies in excess of fifty people. They all know that this is not efficient, but equally they know the importance of democracy. Members wish to feel that they are involved in the management of the organisation, if not directly then by having someone of like mind on the governing body. Special interest groups might be represented by committees but there is the potential for a clash between the views of a specialist committee and the views of the whole organisation. The greater the need to accommodate every conceivable interest through committees and governing bodies the less efficient the trade association will be. Yet at the same time the members will be seeking results and an efficient operation generally. (Boleat, 1996, p. 108)

2.   In his *Life of Julius Caesar*, Plutarch reports the following anecdote. Caesar and his army were crossing a wretched little village in the Alps. While his officers laughed at the misery of the place and laughed at each other, wondering if people were fighting to lead the community, Caesar retorted: "I would rather be first here than second in Rome."

3.   Vladimir Lenin (1906), "Report on the Unity Congress of the Russian Social Democratic Labour Party: a letter to the St. Petersburg workers," accessed 16 March 2020 at https://www.marxists.org/archive/lenin/works/1906/rucong/viii .htm.

5. Dynamic analysis of a business meta-organization

Studies on the costs and dynamics of business meta-organizations are quite sparse. This chapter will attempt to give an original synthesis based on three principles:

1. The financial structure of meta-organizations (revenues/expenditures) must be distinguished from the cost–benefit analysis of collective action. Too often, the two are confused, probably because of the emphasis of the analysis on transaction costs.
2. When studying collective action, a cost–benefit analysis must be conducted, not just a cost analysis.
3. This cost–benefit analysis of the collective action carried out within the framework of a meta-organization must be carried out dynamically. Many studies opt instead for a static analysis. This analysis, however, is different at the time of the creation of meta-organization, its early days, and its institutionalization.

These three fundamental principles being posited, the objective is to explain by dynamic cost analysis a number of phenomena encountered in previous chapters. First is the stability of firms' collective action devices (FCADs) over time, which is greater than that of the member firms, as noted by Bennett (1998). Second is the phenomenon of proliferation already noted by Naylor (1921) – the fact that all sectors and subsectors tend to create a meta-organization intended to represent them, and the fact that for a sector we can have two representative meta-organizations, one of them more specifically representing small businesses in the sector. Finally, it must be explained that meta-organizations can become dormant during certain periods, as McCormick (1996) clearly saw. This is linked to the idea of cycles of political intervention by interest groups (McFarland, 1991). We will begin by analyzing the financial structure of meta-organizations before presenting the elements of a cost–benefit analysis of the collective action and then conducting the dynamic analysis of the life of a meta-organization.

FINANCIAL STRUCTURE OF META-ORGANIZATIONS

There is no comprehensive study of the issue, but the review of the various studies carried out in different national frameworks provides a fairly reliable overview. Lynn and McKeown (1988) have shown that the financial resources of meta-organizations come mainly from membership fees. The proportion is often 80 percent and never falls below 60 percent. For trade associations representing very large industries, trade shows and exhibitions can be an important source of income. They are what Lampel and Meyer (2008) call "field-configuring events." Then come membership meetings, sales of publications, technical and consulting services, and revenue from seminars and training sessions (Lynn & McKeown, 1988, p. 58). Our case study confirms the analysis:

> The budget is relatively simple: 90 per cent comes from membership fees.

Expenses mainly cover staff costs. In his study of British trade associations, Bennett (1998), who, it must be remembered, studied both trade associations and professional associations, estimates that 60–70 percent of association costs are staff costs. However, meta-organizations, trade associations, employ on average many more staff than professional associations, the truly minimalist organizations. These staff are diverse: administrative staff (general secretary or manager, administrative managers, secretaries) and those with more specialized skills (economists, technical experts, lawyers, communication experts). When meta-organizations do market research for their members, they use their own economists or they rent the services of economists from a law firm or a consulting firm. This was the case of the Specialty Steel Industry of North America in the 1980s (Lynn & McKeown, 1988). When meta-organizations have a research center, they employ researchers and engineers, as in the case of the British Cement and Concrete Association in the 1950s, which had a staff of more than 200 people, including staff from its research center (McRobie et al., 1957). These expenses on highly skilled staff can be assimilated to transaction-specific costs. These costs are higher when they are related to lobbying (Bennett, 1998, p. 1371). In our case study, the expenditure structure is as follows:

> Internally, we have 20 permanent staff: a general delegate, a manager in each sub-sector and specific skills (a person on the electrical connection side, a legal officer, a person in charge of economic aspects, and a large communication team – four people). We create about 30 press releases a year, we have a big general symposium, and symposia by subsectors.
> Each year the membership fees for SMEs [small and medium-sized enterprises] are adjusted according to the evolution of their turnover. For us, the main issue of

budget preparation is recruitment. We have been growing steadily for several years. Our expenses are essentially staff costs. The question is hiring an extra person or not. We can make financial reserves. Our situation is very healthy. This is not a source of conflict: we present results and budget to the General Assembly every year and there has never been opposition to the constitution of reserves.

At certain times, the pattern of expenditures may change. For example, in France, an intersector body (livestock professionals and meat professionals) has been created (INTERBEV: Interprofession Bétail et Viande – Livestock and Meat Inter-branch). Because meat consumption is now considered excessive and is receiving increasing criticism in most countries, professionals in the sector are conducting counter-campaigns in the media to encourage eating meat. In 2012, INTERBEV had a budget of 33 million euros and spent one-third on communication activities (in their words, "*porter nos vérités*," or, roughly translated, "sharing our truths"). What this approach highlights is a logic of economies of scope: by sharing the costs, firms can entrust tasks to a meta-organization that they could not carry out alone:

> Put simply, a specialist staff that know the range of issues that local businesses experience and can handle their needs effectively is often a cheap and effective option compared with a business recruiting its own staff or using one-off contracts with consultants. (Bennett, 1998, p. 1371)

The second element is the plasticity of meta-organizations, which can vary their resources and costs. Membership fees make up the bulk of resources (their share almost never falls below 60 percent) and the expenses are essentially staff costs (Bennett, 2000). But resources and expenses may vary depending on the strategy of collective action.

IDENTIFICATION OF THE COSTS AND BENEFITS OF COLLECTIVE ACTION

The structure of revenues and expenditures of the meta-organization gives an idea of the collective action strategy followed, but it does not help us understand this strategy. It requires a more precise analysis of the costs and benefits of organized collective action. Authors (Bennett, 1996; Schneiberg & Hollingsworth, 1991; Taylor & Singleton, 1993) have reasoned in terms of the costs of collective action. They isolated several categories of costs:

- search costs;
- bargaining costs;
- monitoring (or enforcement) costs;
- transaction-specific costs.

Before entering into any collective action, firms must identify the gains they can expect and find a suitable model for collective action. They know that by acting together they are likely to be more effective than if they act in a dispersed way. But, finding the optimal device for collective action can be costly, especially because of the heterogeneity of sectors and their blurred boundaries. These are the search costs. Agreement, especially if the sector is heterogeneous, takes time and sometimes requires significant effort. These are the bargaining costs. If everyone makes the decision for collective action, some may choose to let others act (thereby lowering their costs) while benefiting from the gains of collective action. If everyone has the same reasoning, the collective action fails. Olson (1965) first highlighted the risk of free riding in collective action. Firms must therefore watch each other. These are the monitoring costs. Finally, there are costs related to specific activities that require a specific investment, often in personnel. If the meta-organization produces statistics on the sector, undertakes market research, and conducts lobbying actions, it must hire specialists in these different areas and faces transaction-specific costs.

The analysis in terms of transaction costs provides interesting tools of understanding. Nevertheless, on the one hand, it remains a bit general, it does not take into account costs and benefits jointly, and, on the other hand, it remains quite static (even if dynamic aspects are present – Bennett, for example, notes that the bargaining costs are different before the creation of the meta-organization and once it exists; Bennett, 1998, p. 1370). We will try to simplify the analysis, refocus on the costs and benefits of the firm, and put it into a dynamic perspective. The approach leads us to distinguish costs (direct and indirect) and benefits (collective and individual).

If we adopt what Lawton, Rajwani and Minto (2018, p. 6) call the "member-firm level of analysis", a firm that faces the decision of whether or not to enter a meta-organization faces two types of costs. The first are direct: this is the membership fee. These costs are low in all cases, but we must distinguish between large and small companies. In trade associations and chambers of commerce, the collective interest is to bring together all firms, large and small. The solution adopted is to differentiate the amount of the membership fee according to the size of the company (turnover or number of employees). The small ones pay little and are therefore encouraged to join. In our case study:

> We negotiate the level of contributions permanently. We were well helped by the big firms with whom I had good relations and they agreed to be a little more "taxed" if I may say it, having bigger means. We had membership fees calculated by threshold.

Big companies pay more, but the membership fee remains extremely low compared to their turnover. Moreover, as will be seen in the following chapter, this membership fee generally gives large companies greater voting rights than small firms, which gives them a greater power of influence over the collective decision. If the meta-organization is a club of large companies of different sectors (cross-sectoral meta-organization), bringing together about 20 multinational companies, the costs of membership remain very low. For a multinational group, even the membership fees paid to the multitude of meta-organizations of which it is a member represent a relatively negligible total cost (the CEO of a large international group, during an interview, told us that the financial aspect is "negligible"). These organizations have initial costs and maintenance costs that make them minimalist organizations (Halliday, Powell & Granfors, 1987).

Indirect costs are potentially more important than direct costs and much more variable over time. They are constituted by the time spent by the management of the firm in the activities of the meta-organization according to the status of these managers (top or middle). These are essentially commitment costs (Bonardi, 2008). As we have seen, the meta-organization works through committees. Firms therefore send managers to spend time on these committees and develop common decisions. Here we find the transaction costs. There is a need to agree on positions that will, for example, form the basis of lobbying (bargaining costs). It must be ensured that it is not always the same firms that work for others (monitoring costs). Committee members need to invest in the technicality of the topics covered (transaction-specific costs). Depending on the status of the personnel sent by the firm in these committees, the costs vary. The time spent is valued differently depending on whether it is the president of the company, a vice-president, a director, or a middle manager. The time spent also varies with time. When parliament drafts legislation that may have significant implications for the sector as a whole, some meta-organization committees may work very hard, while in quieter times they meet less often and for shorter periods.

Direct costs are therefore kept low relative to the company's turnover, whether large or small, and they vary little in time (small increases or decreases can be decided from time to time depending on the economic situation). Indirect costs can be high and they can vary considerably depending on the time period. The gains of collective action are first, of course, collective gains. They relate to the reputation of the industry as a whole, which is interdependent with that of the firms that comprise it:

> The reputation of the industry is only as good as the reputation of individual companies. If one company does something wrong, the whole industry can be judged to have done something wrong. (Tucker, 2008, p. 7)

At the same time, it is the purpose of trade association to ensure that the reputation of the industry is greater than that of the firms that make it up. One can speak of a "reputation commons problem" (King, Lenox & Barnett, 2002). The reputation of a sector is the one it has with the stakeholders (customers, suppliers, state, non-governmental organizations [NGOs], etc.) (Winn, MacDonald & Zietsma, 2008). Tucker (2008) viewed the reputational trust of a sector as composed of two interdependent elements: trustworthiness among stakeholders and the capacity of the promise-making. Trustworthiness is related to credibility, integrity, and technical expertise. Insofar as the economies of scope allow a higher collective technical expertise than a company might have, the trustworthiness of a meta-organization can be greater than that of an individual firm:

> An individual or organization could possess technical expertise and exploit information asymmetry to behave opportunistically. However, given the repeated nature of the interaction between a TA [trade association] and its stakeholders, discovered instances of exploiting information asymmetries will lead to longer-term lack of access because of shunning by stakeholders, an outcome obviously deleterious to acting as an industry's reputation agent. (Tucker, 2008, p. 8)

Once trustworthiness is established over time, a trade association is able to issue promises that can be received by the stakeholders. Charters issued by a meta-organization are thus more likely to be accepted as credible than those of a single firm. Once the reputational trust is established, the meta-organization acts as an institutional buffer that protects firms from disturbances in their environment (Miner, Amburgey & Stearns, 1990). In particular, it makes it possible to avoid measures taken by the public authorities that could have a negative effect on the firms in the sector, which these firms would have much more trouble doing individually. And, on a more positive note, it can obtain from the public authorities measures that favor the sector and guarantee it relatively stable resources. But, collective action can also produce individual gains for firms.

As an institutional buffer, a meta-organization produces benefits shared by all firms in the sector, whether they are members of the meta-organization or not. It is not able to provide member firms with an individual competitive advantage. On the other hand, it can provide its members with benefits that non-member firms do not have access to. This advantage is of an informational nature, of the order of what Naylor (1921, p. 128) calls "intimate information." During negotiations with public authorities, during meetings of the meta-organization committees, information is produced that constitutes an "early knowledge of possible trends" (Bennett, 1998, p. 1375). For example, in a sector that relies heavily on public authorities, which is the case for renewable energies, as one interviewee told us, the meta-organization is the first to know that calls for tenders will be launched. In addition, the regulations are constantly changing and the meta-organization has specialists who are in a position to follow these changes and provide information to its members in the form of industry journals, newspapers, or newsletters (Heckman, 2011). As a result, the members are always a little ahead of the non-members, having access to information too complex to be tracked individually, important because of its challenges, and sometimes before this information is made public.

Andrew Grove (1996) showed how a CEO continually seeks to detect and interpret weak signals that come from the firm's environment and that may eventually have an effect on its development ("likely trends"). Meta-organizations constitute for their members one of the places where this detection and this interpretation takes place. For a large company, as noted by the CEO interviewed, it is essential to be at the same time a member of a sectoral meta-organization and of non-sectoral, cross-sectoral meta-organizations that provide access to more diverse information, including issues that have not yet occurred in the sector to which the firm belongs but which are already on the agenda of firms from other sectors. Since the emergence of firms' collective action devices in the late eighteenth century/early nineteenth century, sectoral trade associations have coexisted with chambers of commerce. This co-existence is not a coincidence: the manager of a firm seeks the best knowledge of what is happening in his or her sector and at the same time seeks to know what is happening in other sectors and which could have an impact on his or her business. As stated by this CEO:

> The role of the boss is not to run the shop, but to prepare for the future, so to look at the future, to be attentive to weak signals. If you are too focused on running the business, you have no time. I spend 15 to 20 percent of my time on things like that [participation in sectoral and cross-sectoral meta-organizations] outside the company.

The political benefits can thus be identified as a motivating factor for joining an interest group (Hansen, 1985). There is another individual dimension of participation in collective action, however, which is the empowering feeling of participating in something that goes beyond the usual course of action (Cartel, Boxenbaum & Aggeri, 2019, p. 76). The same CEO states:

> We play in the big leagues to achieve great things.

And, of course, for individuals participating in the work of meta-organizations, the benefit of this participation is the creation of a personal network that makes it easier to solve a number of problems and eventually to manage one's career in the sector outside the area. Our CEO said:

That's how I knew many European bosses.

Finally, the individual gains of the member firms of a meta-organization are the services the latter can offer. Not all meta-organizations offer services, but some have done so for a very long time. In the years 1910–20, Naylor (1921) shows that, for example, the trade associations of certain sectors were able to advise their members on subjects as technical as the insurance costs specific to the activities carried out in a particular sector. In some cases, the handling of insurance matters has resulted in the creation of a captive insurance company (Lynn & McKeown, 1988, p. 45). The range of services possible is quite extensive:

[It] covers information and inquiry services; collective legal, insurance, and pensions services; one-to-one counselling and advice; consultancy; publicity; promotion; employee training; management training; and foreign trade, export promotion, and support. (Bennett, 1998, p. 1376)

This question of services is debated. In fact, the services offered by the meta-organization should be more efficient and therefore less expensive, based on equal resources, than the services offered by the consulting industry on the market, but this is not always the case. Moreover, these services are often more specifically aimed at small firms that are members of the business meta-organization, large companies being able to manage the problem internally with their own resources. As we have seen in this section, the business meta-organizations exist because firms believe that the benefits they bring exceed the costs they generate. But this calculation is part of a dynamic. It is not the same at the time of the creation of the meta-organization and in the different phases of its development.

COSTS AND BENEFITS OF COLLECTIVE ACTION – THE DYNAMICS

The dynamics of a business meta-organization are characterized by a series of turns that we propose to call temporal nodes. The word "node" refers to the idea of branching. These branches can be explicit decisions made by certain actors (like creating a meta-organization) or rather the result of decisions (such as the gradual dormancy of the meta-organization). These temporal nodes are:

- meta-organization or network;
- bricolage or scaling;

- dormancy or activity;
- internal negotiation or new creation.

It is possible to visualize the dynamics of the meta-organization with the schema shown in Figure 5.1.

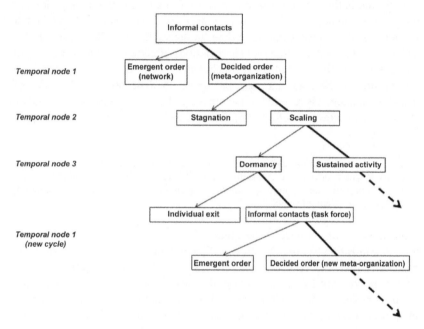

Figure 5.1   The structuring of firms' collective actions

We will study the different temporal nodes from the point of view of cost–benefit dynamics.

Meta-organization Versus Network (Temporal Node 1)

The starting point of the collective action dynamic is the absence of a sector. In our case, France made the significant choice of nuclear energy in the 1970s. It is an inexpensive energy, emitting low greenhouse gas. Under these condi-tions, the emergence of a renewable energy (RE) sector appeared very unlikely or impossible. Only very small niches emerged, occupied by small companies: solar water heaters for swimming pools, new types of wind turbines that fold during cyclones in the West Indies, solar panels to equip isolated houses that cannot be connected to the electricity grid (mountain chalets). The only real market seemed to be the West Indies – there is no nuclear power plant and the usual substitutes (coal-fired power plants) are expensive and polluting. In the early 1990s, RE was an almost non-existent sector:

> At the time, there were seven companies working in the sector and generally overseas for a total of 20 million francs. We started from zero notoriety, from zero public listening. Just this little overseas niche.

> Nobody believed that we could introduce renewable energies; it was not credible. Nobody believed it.

There was a small local trade association (ENERPLAN, limited to the south of France, a very sunny region) of companies that were thinking about the integration of small solar energy devices (solar water heaters, photovoltaic panels) in buildings. It was exclusively in the solar industry. Quite quickly, it became useful to bring in other actors, especially wind power, to talk about renewable energies in general and to try to turn it into a sector. It was at the trade shows and exhibitions that the different firms met. A small network was constituted:

> We found ourselves as friends, without much means, like crazy activists, in a market that did not really exist, that we invented at every step.

But, collective network action (buddies) did not appear as a viable solution, and the idea of creating a collective action device, "beyond" individual actions, emerged then, as explained by one of the founders of the trade association:

> I said to myself: each of us will tinker in his corner, push ideas, so we must create a structure that will carry our aspirations in a way that will be listened to. If we want renewable energy to grow, we must give it a dimension beyond our own activities, we must obtain measures that we will not be obtained individually.

It is the very inexistence of the sector that leads to the creation of a meta-organization supposed to represent this non-existent sector:

> We were so weak that not being together was absurd.

At the same time, the state encouraged these few companies to create a common structure:

> Companies knocked on the door of the government and the minister was tired of seeing them one after the other. The minister told them: regroup and bring together the voice of the industry.

At the beginning of 1993, the French government set up a plan to develop renewable energies in very small niche, isolated sites (mountain chalets, for example) not connected to the electricity grid and too expensive to connect. The aim was to identify these situations and subsidize their electrification mainly with photovoltaic panels. The Fonds national d'Amortissement des Charges d'Électrification (National Fund for the Amortization of Electrification Charges – FACE) was created to help municipalities with less than 2000 inhabitants equip themselves. This plan was announced on 9 February 1993 and the trade association, the SIPROFER (Syndicat des Industriels et Professionnels Français des Énergies Renouvelable – Trade Association of French Renewable Energies Industrialists and Professionals), was created on 24 February 1993. It was a real trade association in the sense that it was national (at the scale of France, and no longer at the scale of a region like ENERPLAN). It had a distinct existence. On the other hand, it did not have any staff, which made it look like the dinner club associations of Galambos (1966), that is to say, a proto-organization. One of the first tasks was to develop a quality charter setting out the criteria for a good electrical installation on remote sites. Operating costs were low:

> We had a little money, in the region of 10 000 euros. We had a small budget, few expenses because no permanent staff.

The meta-organization therefore appeared very weak. However, from the beginning, the two strong points of a collective action device were already present, that is, the roles of institutional buffer and reputational trust. The "sector" (the embryo of a sector) is heterogeneous and some elements pose problems of acceptability (the windmills that suffer from the NIMBY syndrome – Not in My Back Yard!). To speak in terms of "renewable energies" makes it possible to create an institutional buffer, which one of the actors calls an "umbrella":

> We had a renewable energy umbrella with a capital of sympathy, while individually taken, the capital of sympathy is less strong and sometimes there is a capital of rejection (wind turbines).

At the same time, with its limited budgetary means, the trade association began to establish a reputational trust. For very little money, a former senior official offered to write a white paper on RE. This white paper was a turning point:

> We took a real trade association dimension, with power of expression, of proposal, and we obtained the support of the Ministry of Industry. The white paper was the beginning of the SIPROFER mutation. This white paper was devoted to the possibility of renewables. It was sent to politicians, to business. From the white paper,

the idea of a policy became credible. Everyone began to think that something was happening.

The trade association credited the existence of the sector to capital of sympathy, creating both trustworthiness and promise-making in the sense of Tucker (2008):

> We were friendly and not threatening (although wanting to be). So they thought these people are deserving, they exist because there is a trade association. It was politically rewarding for ministers. Today, it's a thing that is accepted, but at the time, people were saying: they are nice, but what they say does not hold, except in the West Indies where there are the trade winds and the sun. We won sympathy. There were people who liked to chat with us, fight with us while remaining political. Quite quickly, the grouping effect had this scope of media and political mobilization.

Before the creation of the meta-organization, a network existed, personal and professional. This network could eventually make a sector exist, but the actors perceived that the dynamics would be a lengthy process. The decision to create a meta-organization appeared very inexpensive and could create a collective dynamic faster and more effectively than the simple network. The direct costs were low: it involved bringing together just six companies and 10000 euros. At this stage, there were indeed no staff to finance. Indirect costs were also low. Search costs were almost zero. Bargaining costs were also very low as it involved agreement between six companies whose leaders were already known to each other. The only indirect costs were the meeting time and, for one of the firms, time spent by its CEO to chair the trade association. There were no committees, so investment time remained low.

The gains appear substantial. The trade association is, by its very existence, an institutional buffer that offers a collective "umbrella" to individual companies. For very low costs, from its first actions of reflection and communication, to a white paper on the future of a real sector, the trade association managed to create conditions of reputational trust. The temporal node is characterized by a cost–benefit balance in favor of creating a meta-organization rather than continuing a network operation. In any case, the model is self-evident: since the nineteenth century, a sector or an industry exists only because it is "represented" by a meta-organization. Naylor presented this phase of the dynamics at the beginning of the twentieth century:

> At the outset the association failed in the support of some of the competitors, but soon secured a majority and proved well worthwhile. So many important matters came up that it was decided to establish an office and employ a secretary. At first the members thought of choosing a secretary from among their own number, but fear of possible prejudice on his part led them to select an outside man in whom they had confidence and who they felt would be perfectly impartial. More frequent meetings

were held. The oftener they met the more they found there was to do. (Naylor, 1921, pp. 9–10)

As the constitutive principle of associations is voluntary membership, this kind of organization is constantly trying to find a balance between the obligation on members to comply with collective rules and the benefits the members receive from the organization (Streeck et al., 2006, p. 2).

Bricolage Versus Scaling (Temporal Node 2)

The first years of the meta-organization show that it is possible to obtain, with very low costs, visible results, as evidenced by one of the co-founders of the trade association, explaining the reaction of the public authorities:

> They exist since there is a trade association.

The question that arises in dynamics is: is this model sustainable or should the meta-organization move to another model, the costs of which are higher but whose benefits can be equally high? The problem is that sustaining the dynamics of the reputational trust involves higher and higher indirect costs:

> We said, we cannot do it, we have our own business.

And, on the other hand, the development of the sector made the big companies start to take an interest in it. The conjunction of the two made the possibility of another model: to move to higher costs (hiring permanent staff) with collective benefits also higher. The choice was therefore to continue in the "do-it-yourself" (DIY/bricolage) or to change scale. A larger company then made a proposal:

> You tinker [*vous bricolez*], you do not do what you have to do. You have to build a real lobby structure with means. If you agree, we take over the bazaar and we will develop it.

The option appeared tempting:

> We were quite flattered that someone brought us such a presence, with a network. But we had not taken into account all the changes it would bring. For us it was unexpected. We will finally have funding, permanent staff.

For small firms, direct costs did not increase and indirect costs decreased. It was no longer necessary for the CEO of a firm to be president of the meta-organization: the big company seconded one of its directors to assume the presidency. The arrival of a dozen big firms allowed the growth of the budgets, a greater notoriety, which caused new adhesions of small and medium firms. Soon, the number of members rose to 400. This increase gradually allowed the hiring of about 15 permanent staff. When the president seconded by the big firm took office, the budget of the meta-organization was 7700 euros. At the end of the scaling phase, it amounted to 3 million euros. The meta-organization accepted all the new members, the only criterion being to pay its membership fees:

> There was no debate on new memberships. Like any other structure that lives off membership fees, the number of members is essential.

Scaling calls for the metaphor (often used in French) of mayonnaise, which has two levels. On the one hand, it expresses the nature of collective action that generates a phenomenon different from individual positions. Mayonnaise is made of individual ingredients (oil, mustard, egg, pepper, salt) that blend into a unified mixture very different from those individual elements that served to constitute it:

> When the mayonnaise has taken, it's impossible to know what is the oil and what is mustard.

But it also expresses the progressive dynamics of the meta-organization in its environment, the reputational trust that characterizes it:

> We have built a reputation among public authorities, journalists, etc. It's all a mayonnaise.

Scaling is marked by the name change of the meta-organization. Our meta-organization was created in 1993 as the SIPROFER. In 1998, it became the SER (Syndicat des Énergies Renouvelables – Trade Association of Renewable Energies). From six companies at its creation, it had grown to 31 members in 2001. Internal rules changed. Large companies pay higher premiums than small firms and, in exchange, have greater voting rights. Step by step, big firms took the lead and the small founding firms lost power:

> I was still vice-president for a few more years. SMEs, we were perhaps stooges, but it was beyond us completely. The one who paid the most had the most votes. Before, it was a man, a voice. There, large companies quickly became the majority.

The big companies brought with them their privileged contacts with the politicians, with the journalists, and the number of permanent staff increased:

> I followed the rise. I was the first employee hired by the association. There were 40 members. When I left, there were five or six employees and 200 members. We ended up having all the energy operators. All joined.

The action was on a scale that did not allow the DIY phase (low costs/positive but limited benefits) and the benefits were important for the sector. The meta-organization was structured into specialized committees whose staff provided the secretariat. However, as the number of members increased, with the entry of the big companies, tensions appeared and the costs of bargaining inside the meta-organization increased:

> We managed to get members, biomass, biofuels; that was very controversial. The president wanted the complete panoply. It's a balancing act.

The direct cost of membership remains low, hence the fact that virtually any firm in the sector becomes a member, but the indirect costs for firms that want to participate actively in the collective action can be significant, especially for smaller or medium-sized firms. They perceive scaling with ambivalence. On the one hand, the mayonnaise has "taken"; the meta-organization has become much more effective. On the other hand, it has changed in nature:

> The trade association has changed dramatically. We went from an SME trade association to a large companies' one. SIPROFER did not take off. The attempt to open up to other companies did not work. We did not have the means, only volunteers. So we accepted.

This ambivalence leads to the question of the next temporal node.

Dormancy (or Apathy) Versus Active Collective Action (Temporal Node 3)

As analyzed by Ahrne and Brunsson (2005, 2011), an organization is a decided order. A meta-organization is an organization in that sense, as is evidenced by the fact that we can identify its date of creation (which is less obvious for a network). Scaling also comes under identifiable decisions: the hiring of the first permanent member of staff of the meta-organization in particular. Temporal node 3 does not belong to highly visible decisions. The meta-organization representing the sector does exist. It produces statistics on the sector, publishes information, organizes training. In this sense, it remains active. Nevertheless, the negotiations with the public authorities are routine and the interest of journalists or NGOs in the sector is low. Gradually, the meta-organization goes into dormancy. This is the phenomenon analyzed by McCormick (1996), one of the only researchers to have studied the dynamics of a meta-organization over a long period: periods of high returns are followed by periods of decline. McRobie et al. had already noted this phenomenon:

> Perhaps the chronic disease of trade associations ... as of trade unions, is apathy. It is not a problem with all associations but the great majority are troubled by it to some degree. (McRobie et al., 1957, p. 188)

The problem is that putting the meta-organization into dormancy is difficult to evaluate from the outside as well as the inside. From the outside, the organization works; it continues to gather its committees and to produce information, to play its role of exchange and conviviality (Spillman, 2012). It is hard to know if it is dormant or not. From the inside, the actors themselves do not necessarily agree on the diagnosis. Some think that the meta-organization continues to produce results, others do not. They can then choose to exit, as was the case for one of the co-founding members of the meta-organization we studied. His diagnosis is as follows:

> The SER has become an unmanageable mammoth. I do not need the collective anymore.

Another metaphor is used, that of the "windmill": the blades continue to spin, giving the impression of an activity, but are in fact empty; they do not involve any internal mechanism that might produce something. The idea is that the costs of bargaining are now so high that the meta-organization is actually paralyzed and that it also does not do much for small businesses:

> [T]he SER has become a general federation, which has trouble expressing clear positions, which has become very legitimist by listening to large companies. The SER has a big congress, but nothing is coming out of it.

For the other co-founder of the trade association, what is wrong is the difficulty of continuing to produce on its promise-making (Tucker, 2008):

> I find the trade association a little absent, not a producer of ideas. The SER is a little lacking in ideas.

From then on, some firms choose to exit and cease to be members. But the exit is very limited: again, because the direct costs are low:

> There were individual exits. It's pretty rare. When they are in, they stay. We did not lose many people. We delivered. We had results; they could not challenge it. The membership fee is money well invested.

And blackmail at the exit is more common than the exit itself:

> Blackmail at the exit, it happens, but it comes mostly from big firms. But we know that big companies have no interest in leaving us. You know, it's a bit of a game of poker.

Even if the meta-organization is dormant, its social function lasts; it can always provide intimate information from time to time (Naylor, 1921). It is not necessary to leave. Some firms leave, often when they are in financial difficulty, but the dormancy of the meta-organization rarely manifests in a massive hemorrhage of members or its disappearance:

> A trade association is often a sort of club, which it is good form to join. Many firms with little genuine interest in the work of the association have not thought of resigning. To belong gives a firm a feeling of respectability, of not being a trouble-maker in the industry. Subscriptions are often negligible as far as a firm is concerned and are paid out of a sort of industrial patriotism. This gregarious feeling may be accompanied by a sense of security derived from membership. Although his firm is not getting anything of value at the moment from the association, a business man may feel that it is there in case of need, and that he ought to help keep it in being as a standby. (McRobie et al., 1957, pp. 180–81)

In times of crisis and dormancy, budgets fall, but not necessarily dramatically. In 1982, a year of crisis for the US economy, 32 percent of trade associations experienced a drop in numbers of staff. For 27 percent of them, the decline was of the order of 10 percent, which is significant without being catastrophic (Lynn & McKeown, 1988, p. 57). In reality, the best indicator of dormancy is more indirect costs:

> Some companies have adopted the practice of sending the same person to a number of committees; often such a person will be someone who is not highly regarded in his own company. (Boleat, 1996, p. 113)

The movement is hardly noticeable. The withdrawal is progressive and it is that that causes the dormancy or accelerates it. The reduction in indirect costs can sometimes precede the effective exit. As explained by a CEO:

> We exit when we see that we do not attend meetings anymore. It means that it does not interest us anymore.

The exit is preceded by a decline in commitment (Bonardi, 2008). It is rare that a business meta-organization disappears, even if it can happen when the sector itself disappears. It is also rare for a massive hemorrhage of members to occur. On the other hand, a business meta-organization can go dormant. The dormancy is characterized by a few exits but especially by a decrease in the indirect contribution of firms: they send middle managers rather than top managers and these managers spend less and less time on the activities of the meta-organization. The same manager attends multiple committee meetings. Ostensibly, the meta-organization goes dormant. It can be reactivated if, for example, the sector is threatened by a law or new policies decided by ministers and parliaments. It is cheaper to reactivate a meta-organization than to rebuild a reputational trust *ex nihilo*.

Internal Negotiation Versus New Creation (Temporal Node 4)

Since scaling has occurred, the costs of bargaining within the meta-organization are increasing; some actors speak of an exponential trend. It is tempting to create a new FCAD. The mechanics of this creation is related to the cost structure. Inside the existing meta-organization, the costs of bargaining have become very high. A small group of firms, two if they are large, a handful if they are smaller, can negotiate more easily and agree on the statutes of a new meta-organization. Once the new meta-organization is created, the cost of bargaining with other interested firms is low: they join or not based on what the small group of firms has negotiated between them. There can be three scenarios: (1) the meta-organization is still active but a new problem arises and the internal negotiations are so long that it is quicker for some firms involved to create a new organization; (2) the meta-organization is dormant and it is more advantageous for a small group of firms that do not find it active enough to create their own structure; (3) some of the members of the meta-organization (a subsector or small firms) feel they are poorly represented in the existing meta-organization and consider creating one that better represents them:

> There were discussions: should we organize as an independent trade association for the solar industry, or join the boiler manufacturers trade association for their technical center?

The option here for this subsector, whose firms informally discuss the solution to be chosen, is either to create a new trade association representing only themselves or to join an already existing trade association. The calculation is clearly a cost–benefit one. And, one of the benefits of joining the existing trade association is the fact it has a technical center, a small structure of expertise that works for its members (individual benefits).

In many sectors, instead of a meta-organization representing the entire sector, there are two. One of which is dominated by large firms, even though it also has small firms (because it is politically costly for a trade association to be only the representative of the major firms in the sector), and the other represents more specifically small firms. In the machine tool industry in the USA we find the National Machine Tool Builders' Association founded in 1902, gathering together 400 firms and claiming to represent 90 percent of the production, and the National Tooling and Machining Association, created in 1943 and counting 3700 members (rather small firms with an average of only 22 employees). In the sector we studied, the association representing all renewable energies, SIPROFER, was created in 1993. It brought together solar photovoltaic, solar thermal and wind energy firms. But in 1996, wind energy companies created their own structure – France Énergie Éolienne (FEE). The subsectors can easily create their own meta-organization, considering that the bargaining costs will be lower in this structure than they are at the level of the meta-organization representing the entire sector and dominated by large companies. Meta-organizations tend to strive to continue to exist (they are characterized by what Spinoza called "*conatus*"), their lifespan is on average very high, and they also tend to proliferate, the creation of a new meta-organization being inexpensive. However, some believe that there is still a minimal cost:

> After that, you need at least one permanent member of staff. You also have to find an independent place to host the new organization (because it cannot be in the premises of a company, otherwise it is too biased). So, there is still a cost of creation.

But, above all, there is a reputational trust to build, the mayonnaise must "take":

> We must build legitimacy. Otherwise, you are two firms that have created something. And the government tells you: what legitimacy? We saw that in the gas industry. A new trade association has been created in which there are some big firms. But I did not see a single article in the press about them. It takes time to gain legitimacy, so that politicians know you.

This is the only barrier, which explains that it is still easier to create a think tank or a club than a real representative meta-organization. Nevertheless, creating a new meta-organization is inexpensive.

CONCLUSION

If one wants to understand the dynamic stages of a meta-organization, its creation, its eventual rise in power, its dormancy, the creation of a new organization by scissiparity, it is necessary to conduct a cost–benefit analysis of collective action. The direct costs, the membership fees, do not explain this calculation by themselves. Indirect costs must be taken into account, that is, the time spent by the managers of the member firms in the activities of the meta-organization, and in particular the bargaining time. On the profit side, we must distinguish the collective benefits, the construction of a reputational trust for the sector as a whole, and the individual profits that the companies can make. These are twofold: first, those that revolve around what Naylor called intimate information, the privileged information from exchanges between members and exchanges between the meta-organization and the constituents of the environment of the sector (public authorities, journalists, NGOs); second, specific services offered by the meta-organization that concern mostly small firms. The evolutionary structure of the costs/benefits of collective action explains in particular why meta-organizations are rather dormant than suppressed, so that they generally persist in their being (*conatus*) as minimalist organizations (Halliday et al., 1987) and why new meta-organizations are regularly created, their proliferation leading to a problem of coordination between them.

CHAPTER SUMMARY

To study the dynamics of FCADs, a longitudinal analysis of a meta-organization was conducted. It was based on the analysis of the costs and benefits of collective action over the long term. For firms, direct costs (fees) are low. Generally, there is a phenomenon of cross-subsidization: large firms pay proportionally more than small firms. The latter therefore pay little. As for large firms, even if their contributions are proportionally higher, they represent very little compared to their turnover. The benefits derived by firms are both individual and collective. The analysis highlights a series of temporal nodes: the creation of a formal organization or the operation of an informal mode; the minimum activity in the DIY or the scaling of the organization; the maintenance of the activity or the entering into dormancy; the possible creation of a new organization. This model explains the proliferation trend of FCADs and, at the same time, their longevity.

6. Activities and strategies of business meta-organizations

Since their inception, firms' collective action devices (FCADs) have had multiple functions, and this is true of trade associations:

> Business associations are oriented to an established, multifunctional portfolio of goals and activities, that as far as we can tell, have also remained basically stable. No single orientation can be used to characterize business associations in general, and most associations express more than one goal. Their expressed orientations included both intra-industry concerns and concerns with influencing the broader public in some way. (Spillman, 2012, p. 106)

The same can be also said of chambers of commerce:

> There is a quite diverse range of factors that lead businesses to want to become members of a Chamber of Commerce: there is no single logic for this form of business organisation. (Bennett, 1995, p. 254)

These devices are actually characterized by a particular combination of multiple activities. Their activities differ from one family of devices to another. Bennett shows that chambers of commerce do little lobbying (only on problems common to all sectors, i.e., very general and cross-cutting problems), while trade associations do more lobbying, defending the interests of a particular sector. In the same way that the array of activities differs from one family of devices to another, it also evolves over time. Japanese trade associations, for example, have played a very important role in helping their members to export in the post-war period. This role has decreased considerably since the mid-1980s (Lynn & McKeown, 1988). Today, Japanese trade associations still exist, but they provide other services. It is therefore understandable that, since their creation, the goals and activities of meta-organizations are not completely clear in the eyes of their members. A few years after its creation in 1906, the first general secretary of the UK Soap Makers' Association stated:

> Truth to tell, the scope of the Soap Makers' Association was never easy to define and probably even its members were far from clear as to what it really was. It proceeded to deal on behalf of the trade with difficulties in the Russian tallow market, it

prepared statistics of raw materials and it argued with public authorities about trans-
port charges and Parliamentary legislation. (Quoted in McRobie et al., 1957, p. 7)

Each FCAD offers its members a unique configuration of activities and services. It is nevertheless possible to categorize these different activities. Staber
and Aldrich (1983, p. 168) identified four: "commercial, public, political, and
solidaristic." But it is necessary to prioritize these categories. The first is the
essential activity: the collection, processing, and exchange of information. An
FCAD cannot exist if it does not provide this function. This solidaristic aspect
is the most visible, and Spillman (2012), for example, focused on this in her
analysis. Then there are non-core activities in the sense that an FCAD can exist
without performing these functions, although in some cases they may play an
important role: member services and general public activity. Finally, there is
a third category of activity that is problematic. This is lobbying, understood in
a broad sense, as "political": "an effort designed to affect what the government
does" (Nownes, 2006, p. 5). This activity is problematic in the sense that it
is controversial: some believe that it is part of the nature of FCADs, their
essence; others that it is only intermittent and that an FCAD may exist (and
even must exist) without ensuring it.

Behind this divergence of analysis, there are two problems. One is methodological: the influence on public authorities often happens behind the scenes
and is therefore not visible. An observer may feel that this activity does not
exist even though it does. The second problem is more theoretical: if it is
a question of influence on the government, is the information game, an essential activity of the FCAD, not already lobbying? Can information be produced
without trying to influence? In this chapter, we will link information collection
and processing and lobbying. But before explaining why, we will deal with
non-core activities of FCADs.

NON-CORE ACTIVITIES

Trade associations, chambers of commerce, and other meta-organizations
representing companies are relatively unknown to the general public because
they do not tend to try to influence or appeal to the latter directly. We have
seen that during some US presidential campaigns, they were able to publish
advertisements but only very large meta-organizations can take this form of
action. The study conducted by Spillman established that point:

> Their attempts to influence public opinion are mostly oriented to specialized
> publics. (Spillman, 2012, p. 340)

In fact, as we saw in a previous chapter and as we will here in more detail, the logic of political influence of the FCAD is mainly a logic of political subsystems:

> The mass public represents but one of many potential venues for a policy debate, and strategic policymakers can often be successful in breaking apart policy-making systems which go against their interests without any direct appeals to the broad public. (Baumgartner & Jones, 1991, p. 1050)

Trade associations generally do not need public appeal to achieve their political goals, and in any case often do not have the means to do so, publicity campaigns being extremely expensive. Nevertheless, today, almost all FCADs have a policy of presence on social networks – in particular, Facebook and Twitter – allowing a wide audience at lower cost.

Direct collective action in the market is almost completely prohibited by antitrust laws (competition policy in Europe). The first trade associations tried to fix prices, to exchange sensitive information on the markets (Yarmie, 1980), and were prosecuted for it (Sklar, 1990). These practices are now forbidden, and the exchanges of information allowed are strictly regulated:

> Current legal advice to trade associations on reporting plans is to avoid collecting data on future prices or production plans, to report data only in aggregate form, and to forgo any attempt to require participation in information reporting programs. (Lynn & McKeown, 1988, p. 47).

Sometimes, however, trade associations are condemned under antitrust laws (or competition policy in Europe). This was the case for the association we studied the year it was created (1993). The electrification market for isolated sites (e.g., mountain chalets) was starting to get organized and businesses, relying on the newly established meta-organization, had divided zones of influence. They were condemned for this by the French antitrust authority of the time, Le Conseil de la Concurrence (Competition Council).[1]

While it is rare for FCADs to intervene directly in the market, there are some possible actions, one of which has been a worldwide success. In 1917, an adman and a former president of the Society of American Florists drank a beer at a Boston café. They were looking for a slogan for the company and came up with, "Say it with flowers!" They did not protect it, however. In 1918, for Mother's Day, the Florists' Telegraph Delivery Association (created in 1910) adopted it for its advertising campaign and it was an immediate success. In 1920, two British florists created Interflora, which grew rapidly around the world using the slogan launched in 1918 by a meta-organization.[2]

Although FCADs rarely campaign directly to the general public or on the market, they often provide services to their members. These services, as we have seen, and this is confirmed by Spillman's (2012) study, already existed in the 1920s and have remained fairly stable: market research, training, insurance advice, legal advice, sometimes a research center or technical center. These services are generally billed to members in addition to their membership dues to the meta-organization. Their contribution to the budget varies but is generally limited. They are also subject to market pressure and competition and often this is a way for large companies to partially subsidize small businesses in order to manage equity and fairness within the meta-organization. In our case study, the trade association does not have a technical center: it organizes for its smallest members one-day training sessions on the evolution of the regulation, it recently launched training on the technological evolutions in the sector (innovation), and:

> So, to provide services: to give them studies, analyses.

Traditionally, the explanation for the service activities to members of trade associations is interpreted as a response to the free-riding problem of collective action (Olson, 1965). For small firms to join the scheme, they must find an individual interest that complements the collective interest from which they could in any case benefit if they were not members. In our interviews, another factor appeared, not mentioned in the literature. The activity of services to members is, for the meta-organization, a way to bring about information and knowledge:

> At the same time, this [the services rendered by the trade association to its members] brings back information from the field. We help and we get information.

If there is little public information available, if direct market intervention is rare, if member services often exist but are a limited activity of an FCAD, specialized information is at the heart of their work. The question arises of whether it can be separated from political influence.

THE CORE ACTIVITY: KNOWLEDGE AND INFLUENCE

A trade association, a chamber of commerce and any other meta-organization, produce, collect, process, and disseminate information. All do not lobby in the technical sense of the term. For Naylor, the two activities had to be clearly separated, with lobbying to be excluded:

> No trade association should ever become a lobbying organization; it should merely see that people are duly informed. (Naylor, 1921, p. 5)

Without going as far as to adopt this position, research has been able to empha-size the role of sensemaking (Spillman, 2012, p. 121) and the purely cognitive role of this type of device:

> [T]rade associations are social arenas that allow members to discuss and debate topics that contribute to overall market discourse. (Kahl, 2018, p. 14)

The question is: is the information and knowledge handled by these organiza-tions pure knowledge, sensemaking, or knowledge that is always intended to influence? Can one, especially in these cases, separate knowledge and power? If not, the creation of an asymmetry of knowledge can be considered as a form of creation of an asymmetry of power (Nicholls & Huybrechts, 2016). It is probably more relevant to consider them as two sides of the same activity, in an approach inspired by Foucault (1980). Indeed, the link goes far back in time. When the National Federation of Associated Employers of Labour was created in 1873 in the UK, its statutes emphasized two aspects: "collect and disseminate throughout the country information bearing upon industrial questions" and "watch over, with a view to influence all legislation affecting industrial questions and the relations of employers and employed" (Yarmie, 1980, p. 229). In trade associations, this dimension is found in other coun-tries such as New Zealand (Reveley & Ville, 2010). And if Bennett (1995) emphasizes that today chambers of commerce do little lobbying, they are born in response to political questions and to influence the decisions of the public decision-makers:

> [C]hambers originated chiefly from an environment of protest against disruptions to international trade resulting from government actions, efforts to reform local government and other institutions, and industrial diversification into complex corporate organizations of proto-global trading companies that were challenging the customary social and political structures. (Bennett, 2011, p. 6)

Just as the boundaries are "tense and permeable" (Alexander, 2006, p. 23) between business and civil society, so they are between cognition and influ-ence. The information policy is always close to the non-market strategy.

NON-MARKET COLLECTIVE STRATEGIES

Since Baron's seminal work (2006, 2016), a field of research has developed on non-market strategies (Bonardi et al., 2006; Dorobantu, Kaul & Zelper, 2017; Lawton & Rajwani, 2015), that is, the strategies carried out by companies to influence their environment: "the social, political, and legal arrangements that structure interactions outside of, although in conjunction with, markets and private agreements" (Baron, 2006, p. 2). Strategies for influencing and controlling the institutional environment have mainly been studied at the enterprise level, but in our societies, the lobbying of a company is generally perceived as direct opposition between public and private interests. Private collective interests, even if they remain suspect, appear more easily legitimate. Imagine the following two situations. In the first, Boeing contacts the president of the US to obtain his or her involvement in a problem concerning the aeronautical sector. In the second, Boeing and Airbus contact the president of the US to obtain his or her involvement in a problem concerning the aeronautical sector. In the first case, there will be a doubt: is it only in Boeing's interests? In the second case, if two companies as competitive as Boeing and Airbus appropriate the political power, it is because it exceeds the interests of a company and affects an important industry for the well-being (welfare) of the country. Collective lobbying is generally much more effective than individual lobbying by a firm. In practice, both can be combined. This collective lobbying, as we have seen, operates relatively little in the setting of the general public. Its natural setting is rather that of subsystems:

> In a pluralist political system, subsystems can be created that are highly favorable to a given industry. (Baumgartner & Jones, 1991, p. 1045)

A subsystem of actors will be formed around a particular industry or activity, including parliamentarians, specialized journalists, officials of the relevant ministries, firms, and trade associations of the industry. It is at the level of this subsystem that interactions and the definition of a policy will take place and the non-market collective strategies will be exercised.

The dynamics of a subsystem is marked by contrasting and alternating periods. The first are periods of routine. The actors know each other, they change little, they exchange information on the functioning of the industry, and collectively define the institutional framework in which this functioning takes place. The second are periods of intense activity. Major policy decisions will be made that can profoundly affect the industry, either positively or negatively. In the latter case, there can be a subsystem collapse:

> We use the term "subsystem collapse" to refer to changes in subsystem organization which enable interests not generally supportive of the involved industry to intrude in the policy process in critical ways. (Baumgartner & Jones, 1991, p. 1051)

These cycles explain why meta-organizations representing a sector may experience periods of near-dormancy (subsystem routine) and periods of intense activity.

These alternations are found in lobbying work, which takes two contrasting forms that Hillman and Hitt (1999) have called "relational political activities" and "transactional political activities." The former consists in developing capital through continuous exchange relations. An American saying goes: "In Washington, DC, if you are not at the table, you are on the menu!" (Ahuja & Yayavaram, 2011, p. 1640). The most visible relationships are with ministers or even presidents or prime ministers, but it is the entire hierarchy of the state apparatus that must be covered:

> Sometimes in trade associations there is a temptation to concentrate almost exclusively on ministers, on permanent secretaries and other top officials. In reality, middle-ranking officials do the bulk of the work. (Boleat, 1996, p. 50)

The latter, transactional political activities, are limited in time and focus on a specific problem. Since their creation, as we saw in Chapter 2, trade associations are linked to bills and acts that can affect a sector, positively or negatively:

> Too often regulatory proposals are introduced in legislative bodies which are the result of a narrow or single point of view that fails to take into consideration the economic and social factors involved. It is one of the functions of the trade association to see that all facts are known and that whatever legislation is passed is based on a complete knowledge of condition, never on personal or class prejudices, nor yet on well-meaning effort to remove deep-seated difficulties by hasty expedients. Reform in the laws is necessary when based on knowledge but under no conditions should laws be enacted without a thorough hearing of all sides of a subject ... it is far better in considering legislation to get the opinion of an association, which is a collective opinion, than that of small groups or of individuals. (Naylor, 1921, p. 5)

To carry out these two types of political activities, two dimensions must be taken into account (Bonardi & Vanden Bergh, 2015). One is specific to the industry itself, and touches on what this industry can get from the policy environment (benefits and costs) and the other is specific to the institutional environment that characterizes this industry (a parliamentary regime different from a presidential one). Lobbying activity itself requires significant capital. Its costs are important:

> High coordination costs, high complexity, and often long duration, as well as the characteristics of high asset specificity and interconnectedness. (Bennett, 1998, p. 1371)

This explains why this activity is mainly concentrated in large meta-organizations. But, there is indeed a link between active, transactional lobbying and relational, the activity of producing information and knowledge.

Because when one turns to transactional lobbying, it is essential to have a good case:

> Influencing opinion formers is not dissimilar from influencing government. It is not a question of elaborate entertaining but rather of ensuring that one has a good case and putting it over well. (Boleat, 1996, p. 55)

Here we come back to what has been said previously: the activity of production of information and knowledge is linked to the activity of influence, without the two being dissociable:

> Information is the key to influencing opinion formers. The same information can be used to influence a wide range of opinion formers and also government. A trade association should always have at its fingertips all of the relevant information about its members and the markets in which they operate. Accurate statistics, well presented and carefully analysed, are a vital part of the information for most industries. A trade association that can control the flow of statistics is in a strong position to influence the public debate. (Boleat, 1996, p. 56)

This intricacy of knowledge and influence is reflected in the implication of trade associations in self-regulation and standardization activities (Barnett & King, 2008; Gupta & Lad, 1983; Lenox & Nash, 2003). For example, by supporting voluntary labeling on products, trade associations can orient firms' behavior towards higher quality and better ethics, thus supporting public policies (which was highlighted in Chapter 3). They play a fundamental role in regulation in general and in the private dimension of regulation (Büthe & Mattli, 2011). As will be seen in Chapter 7, the traditional mechanisms of collective action between firms play a role, for example, in supporting the action of multistakeholder devices. In the next part of this chapter, we will try to show from our case study how the activity of the collective action device is seen by the actors themselves.

CASE STUDY

The study of the core activity of business meta-organizations faces methodological difficulties (see the appendix). On the one hand, researchers never have direct access to lobbying activities. Therefore, the research focuses on the visible, which it is possible to study – for example, political action committees (PACs) (Schuler, 2002). On the other hand, lobbying often results in events not happening, which reinforces its invisibility:

> Also causing difficulty is that many political outcomes are events "that never happened", such as proposed (or even suggested) legislation (e.g., harmful to an

industry or company) that never was acted upon during the legislative session, but
nonetheless is valuable to a firm. (Schuler, 2002, p. 346)

The case study we conducted is based on the facts (the chronology of discussions around the legislative process or regulations, publications related to this
process such as parliamentary debates, controversies in the press) and then on
interviews with the actors.

The Creation of a Meta-organization and a Political Subsystem

In our case study, the interviews produced two apparently contradictory
accounts of the birth of the meta-organization:

> We founded ourselves as buddies, without big means, activists a little crazy, in
> a market that did not really exist, that we invented step by step.

> It was necessary to present ourselves grouped with regard to the public authorities.
> [Question: was it not the government that pushed for the creation of a union?] No,
> they did not push.

> A few firms knocked on the door of the public authorities and the minister was tired
> of seeing them scroll through one after the other. He said: regroup and carry the
> voice of the industry.

In reality, as Naylor had already noted in 1921, it is always difficult to write the
story of the creation of a trade association with precision. Its origins are always
multiple and foggy. What we see in our case study is that the creation of the
trade association coincided almost exactly with the establishment of a public
policy. In 1993, the French government decided to put in place a national
renewable energy (RE) development plan in France to electrify isolated sites
not connected to the electricity grid and whose connection could not be of economic interest, given the removal of these sites from the traditional network.
The agreement was signed on 9 February 1993. On 24 February 1993, the
main French operators working in the field of RE created the SIPROFER,
which became the Syndicat des Énergies Renouvelables (Trace Association
of Renewable Energies – SER) in 1998. Whether the state had formally asked
firms to regroup, or that firms regrouped following the implementation of
a public policy is difficult to reconstruct today, but it is certain that the creation
of the trade association was made in direct connection with the implementation
of a sectoral public policy. The meta-organization was not born from a need for
sensemaking or production of information. It was created directly in relation to
a public policy with the aim of implementing and influencing it.

The Rise of the Trade Association and the First Transactional Lobbying

The first activity of the trade association was on a small scale. At this stage, we cannot really speak of a meta-organization – the organization did not have any permanent or semi-permanent staff. This was more of a dinner-club association. It was in 1998 that the turning point took place. A mid-size company seconded one of its directors to be the part-time president of the association and hired a part-time general secretary as well. The association changed its name and became the SER. The goal set by the new president was to organize a colloquium the following year by involving a minister. To prepare for the colloquium, the only staff member would work on a preparatory document. This document had three basic characteristics. The first was the task of legitimation. In our democratic societies, interest groups are viewed with suspicion. They must therefore legitimize themselves:

> Reflected legitimacy is gained by creating a link in the public mind between the organization and other groups whose goals and activities are seen as aligned with the public interest. (Oberman, 2008, p. 256)

The task here was easy: the Kyoto Protocol had just been signed and it required a reduction in greenhouse gas emissions. Renewable energies were directly part of this general public good goal. In addition, it was reiterated that these energies have a social dimension – they help to bring electricity to isolated communities not connected to networks.

The second characteristic of the document was what it avoided evoking – nuclear energy was hardly mentioned. Knowing that France had chosen massive nuclearization in the 1970s, the meta-organization decided not to attack nuclear power head on. This option was difficult to maintain – the actors of RE, at the time, were often ecological activists and anti-nuclear crusaders. But, the option chosen was political – it would have been dangerous for this small, emerging industry to oppose the powerful French nuclear lobby. Here we find the dilemma of lobbies – they must defend their cause, defending it assumes winning against competing lobbies, but it is often not advantageous to take on these competing lobbies head on. Here, the actors clearly made the choice not to engage in direct confrontation with nuclear power:

> Do not attack neighbors ... do not please yourselves. We do not attack nuclear power.

A compromise had to be made between to "indulge," that is to say, display its anti-nuclear convictions, and to be realistic, that is, to seek to obtain from the government the decisions necessary for the RE sector to develop.

The third characteristic of the document was that it made a request for a change of regulation. So far, the government had launched a call for tenders. The document explained that this regulation did not allow an emerging sector to develop. Indeed, the costs of RE under development were necessarily higher than those of hydroelectric power, for example, the dams having been built in the 1950s–60s and being largely depreciated. The document advocated the adoption of a policy for the development of RE. It proposed the adoption of a system developed in Germany and that other European countries such as Spain and Denmark had already adopted – the obligation for the network to purchase electricity produced by photovoltaic panels at a guaranteed tariff over 20 years.

The first major document produced by the meta-organization was a work of synthesis of the information and the knowledge on an emerging and hitherto little-known sector. But, it accomplished the three fundamental objectives of lobbying: (1) to show that there is alignment between the objectives of the private interest group and the objectives of society, that private interest and public interest are convergent; (2) to manage potential or actual conflict with competing lobbies by trying to avoid direct confrontation; (3) to formulate a clear demand for policy change, building on the fact that other countries were already successfully implementing the requested policy.

The colloquium was the place where knowledge was disseminated to influence both journalists and political circles, a field-configuring event (Lampel & Meyer, 2008). Indeed, the knowledge resonated:

> We were a sounding board. We caught every bit of information and made it resound ... Resound, resound, colloquia, training.

To this extent, knowledge and power were interrelated and their mix created the initiative's success. The trade association's president had experience of the job and an address book that gave him political capital. He succeeded, for the first colloquium of this small trade association, to bring in a minister. For the colloquium of the following year, it was the French prime minister himself (Lionel Jospin) who came and made an important speech on the commitment of France to the RE sector. At the time, the association managed the internal tensions between the different sectors. It was the wind sector that had the lowest costs. Solar was dependent on the solar panels industry, and at that time the costs of panels were very high (prices would start to decline only when Germany started producing on a greater scale and, especially, when China invested heavily in this technology). The association therefore decided to lobby on wind power. It achieved its ends since the government adopted the German approach and put in place for the wind sector the mechanism of the obligation to purchase electricity produced with a guaranteed tariff over 20 years. The meta-organization managed to obtain the regulatory change it had wanted.

The fundamental point for success, however, was a strong technical base:

> I believed and still believe that lobbying by lobbying professionals must be based on solid and professional information, not communication and interpersonal skills. We arrived in ministerial offices and administrations with notes that were ahead of what they had. The government was provided with information that was not available to them. This was true at the Elysée [president's office], Matignon [prime minister's office], central administrations. This has been fundamental. All this was possible only because we had a very precise file, very argued (connection costs, etc.). And we were the only ones to have that.

There, the base was constituted by the document described above. Without this very technical base, nothing could have been done. This is why knowledge and information creating and gathering are the core activities of trade associations. The knowledge the association obtains, in particular from its members, creates an asymmetry with regard to public authorities.

Then the negotiation with government offices became hopeless, "weird," according to an interviewee:

> Meetings at the ministry. The big wind tariff is in 2001. Negotiations are extremely heavy, it's extremely weird, it's like the haggling of carpet dealers. In the end, it's a carpet dealer debate. We asked for 120 cents – we made them scream – we arrived at 83 cents. It's not total nonsense because it's a ministerial ruling. A ruling, it can change. But in reality, Bercy [the French minister of finance] is moving on to other topics and the ruling stands as it is.

One point is important. The outcome of the negotiation should be of a very provisional nature and should be open to question as circumstances change. But, in fact, it is characterized by strong inertia, particularly because politico-administrative life consists of changing subjects of relevance. Government offices move from one topic to another. Abandoned subjects remain in the state that resulted from the negotiations that took place. The negotiations are not called into question unless a crisis occurs. This reinforces the idea that political subsystems are marked by periods of stability and crises.

Relational Activity

The association achieved its first goal: a change in regulations that allowed one of the subsectors, wind power, to develop. It then tried to pursue new objectives, the main one of which was to obtain the same regulatory system for the photovoltaic subsector. The ministry refused, considering that such a device would cost too much. Influence work was therefore put in place, taking the form of continuous contact with ministries and members of parliament:

> Daily [work]: call members of parliament, try to write bits of the laws.

This work does not take place through campaigns aimed at the general public:

> We do not really need public communication. It is very expensive. We do rather ongoing intelligence work.

Rather, the targets are journalists and the work with them takes the form of press lunches:

> We went through the big journalists. Press lunches. Chez Françoise.[3] A dozen journalists. Their questions were answered. They must be informed.

Influence is based on creating an imbalance in terms of information and knowledge:

> At the ministry, the guy responsible for renewable energy was on his own with half a secretary, and there were 15 of us.

The game of negotiation is presented by one of the presidents of the meta-organization and is analogous to judo. It is the state (ministers, parliamentarians) that makes the decisions; it is the state that holds the power. But, as in judo, the strength of the opponents can be used to destabilize them and maneuver them into the required position. If mass media campaigns have not been used, less expensive forms of public action than advertising campaigns have been considered. For example, wood is one of the RE subsectors. A French member of parliament made a statement that, for him, wood heating was only ornamental, for show. In reply, the meta-organization organized a vast national photo contest of wood heaters to show him how widespread this type of heating is in France and that it is used in a utilitarian way and not just for the joys of firewood in second homes.

Moreover, the SER is obviously present today on social networks. In particular, the tool can be used, in combination with more traditional means such as reports posted on the Internet, to counter rumors or fake news aimed at the general public, such as infrasound emission by wind turbines causing ear injuries or cancer. The collection and processing of information, the establishment of a knowledge base on the various aspects of the sector, constitute substantive work that prepares for the transactional action when a change in the political cycle makes it possible or requires it. In the game of these two activities, a weakening factor can be the division between multiple meta-organizations.

In our case study, the division between the SER, representing all subsectors, including that of wind energy, and FEE was a weakness, as explained by a representative of SER:

> I met the representatives of FEE, at the cabinet [of the minister]. FEE was smaller. Facing the minister, it is very dangerous to have two representatives. The minister wanted to know if there were any differences between them.

This division was overcome during the critical period after the FEE joined the SER (in 2005) and became its wind power committee. Then, the two meta-organizations separated again (2012).

New Transactional Action

As was mentioned earlier, in the years following obtaining the new regulatory mechanism for wind energy, the trade association tried to obtain the same measures for photovoltaics, but without success. The costs of such measures appeared prohibitive for French public finances. But, in 2005–06, the government of Dominique de Villepin, then prime minister, faced difficulties. In August 2005, the government introduced the "First Employment Contract" (Contrat de Première Embauche – CPE) system.[4] During the fall of 2005 and the beginning of 2006, these measures aroused strong opposition from the unions. The government was weakened and the prime minister was looking for ideas to be able to turn the page and move to another phase:

> The takeoff of photovoltaics in France is the attempt by Villepin to get out of the CPE crisis. As prime minister, Villepin got stuck in 2005–06. 2005, CPE was a disaster. He got burned. He was prime minister, his request was: find an idea. One of his advisors suggested a boost on photovoltaics. We had been asking for years and the ministry of finance was blocking it. You have to be ready, to lobby. We had seen dozens of ministers, parliamentarians, journalists, we had the colloquium. From time to time, it works. The solar, we had prepared everything, and Matignon called us.

A trade association must be ready, must have technical records so that it can respond to a political need that may appear very suddenly. Relational and transactional subsystems are therefore interwoven with each other. In our case study, the sudden political change made it possible to set up an industry-friendly system. But there can also be crisis situations:

> Crisis management exists in this kind of organization; we did not know that much. There, you have to be in defense.

If the sector has not experienced a real crisis, it is subject to constant attacks. A number of French parliamentarians are extremely opposed to onshore wind energy. They believe that it cannot replace nuclear power and destroy the landscape. They have formed a small "Vent de Colère" (Wind of Anger) interest group that is lobbying parliament and ministries to minimize the development of wind power. The SER must continuously monitor the initiatives of this interest group that is opposed to wind energy.

The Risk of Too Much Success

To the extent that the trade association has the best information and knowledge of the industry, it can go too far in its judo game with the state:

> The only time when the management of the information could be delicate is the moment when you say to yourself: I negotiated too well; it is a little too favorable.

This is indeed what happened in the photovoltaic business (Debourdeau, 2011; Dumez & Renou, 2018). The trade association has succeeded in getting the German system transferred to France – the obligation of the network to purchase electricity produced by photovoltaic panels at a guaranteed rate over 20 years. But, the German system provided for two accompanying measures: first, the progressive lowering of tariffs, since the developing sector had to make economies of scale; then a biannual follow-up of the evolution of the costs that can lead to a reduction of the tariffs. These two measures have not been transferred into the system set up in France. The regulator of the energy sector, the Commission de Régulation de l'Énergie – CRE (Energy Regulatory Commission) had drawn the government's attention to the risk presented by the decisions taken, but it fell on deaf ears. However, a few years after the adoption of the new device, Chinese industry exported solar panels at low cost. As a result, guaranteed rates became incredibly rewarding. A bubble occurred:

> Prices for solar panels made in China fell in a very short time. It caught everyone short, including me. The tariff had become too advantageous. There was a great imbalance of information. This is something I learned. The final decision maker is under the pressure of circumstances. His administration does not necessarily have the information. The closest are companies. There, the guy knew he could buy a Chinese panel at one-third of the German one. Of course, he did not say it. The professional organization only picked up the info late and was not supposed to go to the public authorities and say, lower the tariff.

The trade association was the first to acquire the information that showed that the tariff that had been negotiated was too advantageous because of the significant price reduction of photovoltaic panels of Chinese origin. Some of its membership were involved in the speculative bubble, it was difficult for the association to alert the authorities and they remained in the dark for several months, leaving the bubble to develop. In December 2010, the government decided to block all projects. Subsequently, the system of the purchase obligation with a guaranteed tariff was abandoned and France returned to the system of calls for tender.

The Bouquet (a Bundle of Activities)

As mentioned earlier, FCADs have two core activities: information gathering and processing on the one hand, and less essential but important activities, such as services to members, on the other. One of the presidents of the meta-organization we interviewed speaks of a "bouquet":

> The strength of the trade association: a bouquet of skills, both interactive and unique. We provide services to members in addition to lobbying and communication. We render technical services.

For example, the SER organizes information days on calls for tenders. More recently, the theme of innovation has emerged as an important one:

> We understood that innovation was an important subject. We will create a new transversal committee, industry and innovation. The decision was made, we will appoint the chair of this committee to the next board of directors. This commission will take care of innovation in all sectors. It will organize meetings. This initiative came from listening to the members. We can see the rise of the issues of integration of renewable energies on the network, storage, where it moves strongly, etc. Members have real information needs, and more than that, on these issues. We want to provide them with a state of the art.

The services are intended for small member companies. Indeed, as noted by one interviewee:

> All large companies have their innovation policy.

And, as always, the question arises of the relationship between the big members and the little ones:

> We will have to organize the relationship between the innovation policy of the big and the collective. It will rather bring to the attention of members the state of the art on storage, smart grids, etc.

The "bouquet" allows the meta-organization to have an overview of what is happening in the sector, a distributed knowledge in the sense of Girard and

Stark (2002). What matters is the complementarity of activities and the diversity of sources of information that it allows.

CONCLUSION

The analysis of the activity of the organization we studied specifies certain aspects with regard to the activities of the trade associations and of the political activities of the firms. There is a need to prioritize the activities of meta-organizations between core and secondary activities. Next, there is the link between knowledge production and lobbying or influence work. The task of a meta-organization is to "resonate" the information, as one of our interviewees says, and to create an imbalance between the meta-organization and the public authorities, which allows a negotiation practice that is close to judo.

CHAPTER SUMMARY

Since their inception, FCADs have undertaken multiple activities, changing over time, each FCAD offering its members a particular bouquet of activities. Certain activities are prohibited by antitrust laws (exchange of information on prices or market shares, coordination of strategies). Two activities are essential: the collection and processing of information, and influence or lobbying. Both are intricate: information and knowledge are treated according to influence. There are few campaigns aimed at the general public. Influence is at the level of the state (in all its components: ministers, parliamentarians, civil servants) and that of journalists, often specialized. It is operated at the level of a political subsystem. With regard to dynamics, two phases must be distinguished. In the relational phase, information is regularly given to officials, ministers, parliamentarians, and journalists. The transactional phase is a time when the meta-organization can make the state adopt a measure favorable to the industry or, on the other hand, must protect the industry from a measure that could have a direct negative impact on it.

Our case study confirms these elements. The creation of the meta-organization we studied was concomitant with the creation of a public policy related to the sector. The study shows that the role of meta-organization is to "resonate information" and that the influence results from the establishment of a dissymmetry of knowledge between the state and the meta-organization.

NOTES

1. Conseil de la Concurrence, Décision No. 03-D-54 du 28 novembre 2003 relative à des pratiques relevées sur le marché des énergies renouvelables.
2. Naylor (1921) and O'Keefe (2019).
3. Chez Françoise is a well-known Parisian restaurant, expensive but not too extortionate. A journalist we interviewed told us that the professional from the wind energy association invited journalists from major newspapers to Drouant, a Parisian restaurant even better known than Chez Françoise, to talk to them about the problem of the lack of development of wind turbines in France.
4. This employment contract, available only to employees under 26, would have made it easier for employers to fire employees by removing the need to provide reasons for dismissal for a trial period of two years. There were massive protests and this amendment to the Equality of Opportunity Act (Loi sur l'Égalité des Chances) was rescinded.

7.   Other types of firms' collective action devices

The two prototypical forms of FCADs are the trade association (which gathers the firms on the basis of the same activity, of a sector) and the chamber of commerce (which brings together firms of all sectors on a territorial basis – city, region, country, or even global in the case of the International Chamber of Commerce). But, as we have seen, these two organizational forms are only prototypes in Wittgenstein's (1953 [2008]) sense, families of collective action devices being diverse. In the recent period, collective action devices have arisen in which firms are present but in addition to other classes of actors (states, non-governmental organizations [NGOs], universities, etc.) – in essence, multistakeholderism. How to explain this emergence of new devices of collective action? It is mainly related to the development of meta-problems (Cartwright, 1987) or "wicked problems" (Dentoni & Bitzer, 2015; Dentoni, Bitzer & Schouten, 2018) such as environmental issues, human rights, sustainable development, and bribery. These types of problems are characterized by the fact that they have a public dimension, that they are complex, that they provoke a confrontation of values, and that they require a collective solution. Indeed, to try to solve such problems, it is necessary to increase the diversity of repertoires, gather a variety of perspectives (Seidl & Werle, 2018), knowing that these perspectives must not only be of a cognitive dimension but that they also must reflect a diversity of values, as emphasized by Cartwright (1987).

INTRODUCTION TO MULTISTAKEHOLDERISM

We define multistakeholderism as two or more classes of actors engaged in a common governance enterprise concerning issues they regard as public in nature, and characterized by polyarchic authority relations, constituted by procedural rules. (Raymond & DeNardis, 2015, p. 573)

It quickly emerged that only one class of actors, the companies, could not claim to provide solutions to meta-problems. We have seen the development of multistakeholderism, not only including firms, but also other private actors such as NGOs and associations, as well as individuals:

> Multi-stakeholder networks have caught public attention since the mid-nineties. In these networks actors from business, civil society and governmental or supra-national institutions come together in order to find a common approach to an issue that affects them all and that is too complex to be addressed effectively without collaboration. (Roloff, 2008, p. 234)

Multistakeholderism takes place in the regulatory process, especially where there is a gap in the regulation, either for emerging issues or for complex issues that cannot be solved individually. It is a dynamic process, as shown by Roloff. It follows a sort of lifecycle, punctuated by agreements, and can eventually "die." Initiatives may take the form of voluntary programs of action (Fransen, 2012). The means of action include codes of conduct and standards developed around them. Indeed, in the 1980s and 1990s, firms began to publish their own codes of conduct – for example, in the field of corporate social responsibility (CSR) or labor rights (Utting, 2002). Then, in the 1990s, when meta-problems were aggravated, many codes were formulated by trade associations (the phenomenon was not new, as Naylor had already described it in 1921). In 2000, a study conducted by the Organisation for Economic Co-operation and Development (OECD) identified, for example, 246 codes of conduct around the issue of bribery. 118 came from individual firms, most from other business associations (Gordon & Miyake, 2000). As the study showed, this situation led to a great variety of codes and inconsistencies between them. The solutions provided by companies and trade associations were therefore unsatisfactory. Such codes are not only simply mechanisms by which various stakeholders attempt to govern the action of the corporation but also systems by which each stakeholder attempts to gain or retain some legitimacy (Mele & Schepers, 2013). Another problem arose. All these codes were based on self-regulation and the "trust me" attitude:

> Through corporate self-regulation, companies were adopting what Shell and some other companies later acknowledged was an ineffective "trust me" attitude, which called on stakeholders to simply take them at their word (Dommen, 1999). Sceptical stakeholders soon came to demand that companies actually "tell me", "show me" or "prove it" via environmental and social reporting, independent monitoring, verification and certification systems. (Utting, 2002, p. 7)

A structure of the a-hierarchical type (called heterarchical or polyarchical) is then set up, which follows procedural rules to try to find solutions to these problems. For multistakeholderism to be possible, at least two distinct classes of actors must be brought together in the organization. Four classes of actors can be isolated: states, formal intergovernmental organizations (IGOs), firms, and civil society actors. We can then identify eleven forms of multistakeholder organization (Raymond & DeNardis, 2015, p. 583):[1]

- states, IGOs, firms, NGOs;
- states, IGOs, firms;
- IGOs, firms, NGOs;
- states, IGOs, NGOs;
- states, firms, NGOs;
- states, IGOs;
- states, firms;
- states, NGOs;
- IGOs, firms;
- IGOs, NGOs;
- firms, NGOs.

As we see, only seven of these organizational forms involve companies:

- firms, states, IGOs, NGOs;
- firms, states, IGOs;
- firms, states, NGOs;
- firms, IGOs, NGOs;
- firms, states;
- firms, IGOs;
- firms, NGOs.

These forms are emerging ("inchoate," in Raymond and DeNardis's words) and all of them have not been studied. In fact, we can sometimes find classes of actors that have not been identified by Raymond and DeNardis, such as universities and research organizations (which can be classified in the category "civil society" but also in another category: "organizations of expertise"). In this chapter, we will not explore the full diversity of all these possibilities but take two cases and try to analyze them using the theoretical elements that have been presented in the preceding chapters.

THE UNITED NATIONS GLOBAL COMPACT (UNGC)

Presentation

The idea of the Global Compact was launched at the Davos forum on 31 January 1999 by UN Secretary-General Kofi Annan, advised by Chief Executive Officer (CEO) Stephan Schmidheiny. Kofi Annan addressed private companies with the following speech: "You do not need to wait for governments to pass new laws. You can and should act now, in your own self-interest. The sustainability of globalisation is at stake" (Ruggie, 2002, p. 28). Officially, the pact was created on 26 July 2000 at the UN. Ten principles were formulated relating to human rights, the environment, forced labor, child labor, discrimination, and bribery. Companies should make three commitments:

- to adopt the ten principles;
- to publish a report once a year showing the initiatives they have taken to apply these principles, explaining their difficulties and working to define best practices;
- to develop projects with partners applying the principles, especially in countries that have remained marginalized from economic and social development (Ruggie, 2002, p. 31).

But, if the device targets companies, it causes three groups of actors to interact: government, businesses, and civil society and labor organizations, with a multiplicity of subcategories: academic, foundation, public sector organizations, global business associations, local business associations, global labor, local labor, small or medium-sized enterprises, cities, global NGOs, local NGOs, companies. In total, the UNGC brings together more than 9500 players, the vast majority of whom are companies.

Since 20 April 2006, a board has presented itself as "a multi-stakeholder body, providing ongoing strategic and policy advice for the initiative as a whole and making recommendations to the Global Compact Office, participants and other stakeholders." It consists of four constituency groups: business, civil society, labor, and the UN. The UNGC is funded both by state contributions to the UNGC Trust Fund and corporate contributions to the Foundation for the Global Compact. The budget is mainly used to finance the UNGC Local Networks.

Analysis

The UNGC has a number of similarities with other collective action devices involving companies. Organizations decide "[to combine] their efforts voluntarily to achieve their goals." Collective action is voluntary and "rests on bargain, not coercion" (Ruggie, 2002, p. 33). There is a small hierarchical structure that ensures the coherence of the action and serves as support for its functioning. There is therefore an articulation between heterarchy and hierarchy.

The peculiarity of the device comes first from the fact that it combines heterarchy and hierarchy in a particular way. The president of the board, in fact, is not elected – it is the secretary-general of the UN who performs this function.

Another point is that the office (the hierarchical part of the meta-organization) is very small in relation to the number of members. Originally, the head office had only three people, Georg Kell, John Ruggie, and Denise O'Brien, which was very few "to juggle the conflicting interests of the initiative's participants" (Kell, 2005, p. 69). Another difference is that members are heterogeneous categories. In a chamber of commerce or a trade association, the members are all companies. We have seen that within this group, there is a certain heterogeneity between large and small firms, between producers and distributors, and so on. But this heterogeneity is not of a statutory nature. Here, members belong to different categories, "business" being one of them. In this category, there are both companies and trade associations. The device therefore uses the capabilities of other collective action devices in addition to more traditional firms. This is notably the case for the actions of local networks that have interacted with several traditional business meta-organizations (the International Chamber of Commerce, Prince of Wales International Business Leaders Forum, International Organisation of Employers, and the World Business Council for Sustainable Development; Ruggie 2002; Williams, 2004).

There are no committees either, but there are about 100 local networks that conduct "learning exchanges, information sharing, working groups" and "partnerships and dialogues that tackle issues specific to local contexts" (Raymond & DeNardis, 2015, pp. 601–2). As for its essential activity, the UNGC is analyzed as "a platform for dialogue and learning" (Rasche & Gilbert, 2012) or a "learning forum" (Ruggie, 2002, p. 32). The lack of monitoring has been strongly criticized (Sethi & Schepers, 2014). One point has been less emphasized: it is the work of developing indicators – for example, in the field of human rights – that is the central element of what Westerman (2018) has called "outsourcing the law," and Merry (2011, p. 585) "a technology for reform." For example, in the area of human rights, the two principles are extremely general: (1) businesses should support and respect the protection of internationally proclaimed human rights; (2) they should make sure they are not complicit in human rights abuses.

How can companies explain what they are doing concretely to apply these two principles and particularly to show in each annual report how they have progressed in the application of these two principles? The advice given to them is: "to use performance indicators for your company's size, sector and single operating environment, and also allow for benchmarking and comparability" (UNGC, 2008, p. 15). In practice, the indicators are developed at sector level (and here trade associations play a central role), often in collaboration with universities and NGOs; the indicators being developed by a single company might not be legitimate and may be strongly challenged. UNGC as an organization essentially produces principles, indicators, and a benchmark of best practices.

OFFICE FRANCO-ALLEMAND POUR LA TRANSITION ÉNERGÉTIQUE (OFATE)

Presentation

The Office Franco-Allemand pour la Transition Énergétique (Franco-German Office for Energy Transition) was created in 2006 as the Bureau de Coordination Énergie Eolienne (Wind Energy Coordination Office) by the French and German governments. In 2013, it became the Office Franco-Allemand pour les Énergies Renouvelables (OFAEnR – Franco-German Office for Renewable Energies) before being finally transformed in 2016 into the OFATE. The OFATE deals with wind energy, photovoltaic solar energy, biogas, and cross-cutting issues related to the energy transition. It has over 200 members, large and small companies, operating throughout the energy sector, trade associations, academic institutions, and organizations representing civil society (NGOs such as Greenpeace). Diversity of the members is sought for knowledge reasons (e.g., agriculture was not greatly represented and an effort was made to attract actors from the agricultural world concerned with energy issues). It is a kind of platform for information exchange and networking.

The 200 members form the general assembly. The general assembly elects a college of organizations and a college of companies.[2] The two states form the third college as benefactor members. The three colleges form the steering committee with 21 members and each has one vote (called group voice). This steering committee appoints the directing committee (two people, the director, and his or her deputy). The same person is director and president of the general assembly. The budget is provided by the two states (38 percent), by the membership fees (48 percent), the rest being provided by paid services. Both states have a veto right. The scale of contributions is very flat (900 euros for research organizations and from 1500 to 6000 euros for companies depending on their size) and each member has one vote (big companies do not pay contributions substantially higher than the small ones and have no particular weight in the votes).

The OFATE produces general public information (for example, studies on topics related to renewable energies, comparing, for example, legislation in France and Germany) and studies reserved for members (for example, translations of French legal texts into German and vice versa, or synthesis notes). Studies never include recommendations to governments. They are only informative and analytical. The lobbying dimension is therefore deliberately discarded.

Analysis

Again, there are provisions that resemble the classic devices of collective action involving companies, including trade associations, and others that differ. One sees members who pay a fee, who elect representatives, with a heterarchical part (the steering committee) and a hierarchical part (a staff headed by the director and his or her deputy, composed of seven people in the Paris office and seven in Berlin). The organization essentially produces information, divided into information reserved for paying members and general public information. Each year, it processes about 250 requests from its members.

There are also differences from traditional structures. For example, the heterarchy/hierarchy link is distinctive since the director of the staff is also statutorily the chairperson of the general assembly. The members are grouped into separate colleges, and the status of one class of members, the two states, is exceptional in that they have a veto right. Each member has one vote in each college, but each college has a group voice. Originally, there were only two colleges: that of the states and that of the firms, each having one voice. The Charlottenburg court has imposed the creation of a third college to prevent the possible block of one vote against one. The organization does not have standing committees. It can create working groups, but this possibility, provided by the statutes, has never arisen to date. The essential activity is information, whether for members only or for the general public.

The operation illustrates what has been said previously about direct and indirect costs in Chapter 5. In the beginning, companies thought that the OFATE could have a lobbying role. They joined and sent representatives to participate in the general assembly and steering committee meetings. Pretty quickly, they understood that it was only a structure of exchange and information. They continued to bear the direct costs (very moderate membership fees) and reduced their indirect costs (with lower attendance of their managers at meetings). The OFATE thus illustrates the fact that a collective action system can operate without lobbying activities, simply as a platform for exchange and information. In this case, the companies accept the direct costs (low), that is to say, they pay their fees and join as members. On the other hand, they limit their indirect costs as much as possible, that is, they send only middle managers and not senior executives to meetings organized by the organization, and limiting their time involvement. Moreover, the case of the OFATE shows that, in multistakeholder systems, the president tends not to be elected. Indeed, it seems difficult to elect a president jointly by state representatives, representatives of enterprises, and representatives of NGOs, particularly because of the special status of states. Members then tend to find a solution other than election, but nevertheless respecting the spirit of heterarchy. This problem is found in other multistakeholder devices. For example, the Voluntary Principles on Security

Table 7.1   *Traditional meta-organization versus multistakeholder organization*

Characteristics of the Meta-organization	Trade Association	UNGC	OFATE
Chairperson	Elected by the members	Non-elected (UN secretary-general)	Elected by the steering committee: director of the staff and chairperson of the general assembly
Board	Reflecting diversity of members	Reflecting diversity of members	Steering committee reflecting diversity of members
Members	Undifferentiated	Classes of members (government group, businesses, civil society and labor organizations)	Classes of members (states, organizations, firms; the two states have a veto right)
Groups	Permanent and transitional committees	Local networks	No permanent committee, transitional committees and work groups are possible but not effective
Main activities	Information and lobbying	Learning forum Outsourcing the law (designing indicators)	Information and analysis
Secondary activities	Organizing workshops and conferences Services to members	Organizing workshops and conferences	Organizing workshops and conferences
Financing	Firms' fees Paid for services	Private and public funds	Private and public funds

and Human Rights (VPSHR) is a system of states, mining companies, and NGOs to ensure that human rights are respected when companies ensure the safety of their facilities. The presidency is rotating, with one of the participating states taking over the presidency of the organization for one year and passing the baton to another the following year.

Table 7.1 compares the characteristics of traditional meta-organizations such as a trade association with those of the two multistakeholder meta-organizations we studied, the UNGC and the OFATE (see above).

FIRMS' COLLECTIVE ACTION DEVICES AND PLATFORMS

Collective action between economic actors has undergone a profound and visible evolution in recent years with the emergence of platforms (Amazon, Uber, etc.). A German journalist, Sascha Lobo, talked about "platform capitalism" (Lobo, 2014). In response, other authors have referred to the development of a "platform cooperativism" (Scholz, 2017), technology allowing platforms to function as worker cooperatives. Can the technological dynamics of the platforms upset the traditional FCADs that have organized the collective action of firms since the end of the nineteenth century – trade associations and chambers of commerce? As we have seen, trade associations and chambers of commerce all have a website on which they have developed information and exchange services, and they use social networks to make communication. But the question that must be asked is different: can platforms be created that would replace the traditional forms of collective action between firms?

In a previous chapter, we identified two basic types of activity for trade associations and chambers of commerce: core activities, subdivided into two, lobbying and information, and secondary activities, including member services, R&D, training, standardization, and so on. It is very likely that platforms could appear around the creation of secondary services for companies belonging to the same sector or cross-cutting platforms offering, for example, services to small companies. No doubt there already are some. It is likely that platforms may exist to manage the collection, processing, and dissemination of information at the sector level or, in the same way, for small or even large firms, sharing information needs – for example, on specific public policies. The OFATE is quite close to what would be the model of a platform of this type. These platforms could be capitalist ones (private operators) or cooperatives (owned and managed by firms in the same sector, for example), or even like the OFATE and the UNGC, benefiting from public funds. It is more difficult to see how a platform could provide lobbying activities.

But can we reason activity by activity? What the history of trade associations and chambers of commerce shows, and what our case study does also, is that these devices of collective action between firms have always been based on a bundle, a package or a "bouquet" of activities, a "multifunctional portfolio of goals and activities" (Spillman, 2012, p. 106). If this bundle could evolve over time, and if it continues to evolve, it remains as a bundle. We looked for platforms that replaced these very old types of organizations such as trade associations and chambers of commerce and we did not find them. The reverse takes place: these traditional organizations tend to integrate the dynamics of platform technologies to develop new activities. On its website, for example, the Paris Chamber of Commerce and Industry has a range of business services offered, some free and others paid for, for its members and for non-members. This movement appears general: traditional organizations of collective action between firms have rethought and reorganized some of their activities through information and communication technologies. But, it seems they continue to offer a specific bundle of activities that protects them from being a platform.

CONCLUSION

In the recent period, there have been FCADs whose firms are members but only form one category of members among other categories (states, NGOs, universities, etc.). These organizational forms are moving away from the traditional prototypes of collective action, trade associations and chambers of commerce, but share certain characteristics with them: they are a matter for collective action, companies are members of them, they produce information about companies and participate in the dissemination of good practices. They articulate heterarchy and hierarchy, but in original forms. These devices complement the traditional devices, covering fields of action in which these traditional devices lack legitimacy, and at the same time rely on them. In the case of the UNGC, for example, the International Chamber of Commerce has played an important role in its development, and trade associations are involved in local networks; in the case of the OFATE, there are companies and trade associations among the members. More than a radical organizational innovation, these FCADs represent a broadening of the family of collective action devices involving companies.

CHAPTER SUMMARY

Meta-problems (environmental, human rights, sustainable development, etc.) are not new, but they occupy a growing place on the agenda of public and private action. Traditional FCADs, trade associations and chambers of commerce, are involved in solving these problems. Firms are not sanctioned to deal with these problems alone. In the recent period, therefore, multis-takeholderism has developed. Devices have emerged bringing companies together with other classes of actors: states, trade unions, universities, and NGOs. The study of two devices of this type, the UNGC and the OFATE, shows that these devices articulate heterarchy and hierarchy, as trade associations and chambers of commerce also do, but in a different way.

One may wonder whether the traditional mechanisms of collective action between firms, the trade associations and the chambers of commerce, could undergo a form of uberization. It does not seem to be the case at the moment. This is perhaps due to the characteristic of this type of organization that, since the nineteenth century, functions as a bundle (or bouquet) of various activities, these activities being able to vary in time and according to the sectors without the existence of a bundle be questioned. On the other hand, trade associations and chambers of commerce have integrated platform logic into their activities (in terms of information processing and services offered to their members).

NOTES

1. As the organizational dimension is sometimes minimal and there is always a public dimension to the issues discussed, some speak of Global Public Policy Networks (GPPNs; Reinicke, 1999–2000). The three major examples are: the Global Reporting Initiative (GRI), the Extractive Industry Transparency Initiative (EITI), and the United Nations Global Compact (UNGC).
2. A reform is envisaged to transform the college II into a college of scientific organizations, with college III regrouping the companies and the NGOs, and college I remaining that of the states.

Conclusion

Existing research on firms' collective action devices (FCADs) is very dispersed. Some researchers are interested in trade associations, others in chambers of commerce, others in multistakeholderism, some develop a historical vision, others do not. Consequently, these studies lead to fragile theoretical generalizations.

This book is based on an idea borrowed from the philosopher Wittgenstein ([1953] 2008). To study certain phenomena, even before attempting a theory, one must give an *"übersichtliche Darstellung,"* a synoptic view or a "perspicuous representation." Faced with a complex, multifaceted phenomenon, this is the first and fundamental step – first, we must give as complete a picture as possible of the diversity of the phenomenon:

> A perspicuous representation produces just that understanding which consists in "seeing connexions." (Wittgenstein, 1953 [2008], §122, p. 42)

Too often, researchers have wanted to report on the collective action of companies based on research on a trade association, or on a chamber of commerce, or on a multistakeholder organization, that is, on a unique form of meta-organization. By not taking into account the possible diversity of the phenomenon, these studies resulted in false generalizations, that is, true generalizations on part of the phenomenon without realizing that a broader view was necessary:

> A main cause of philosophical disease – an unbalanced diet: one nourishes one's thinking with only one kind of example. (Wittgenstein, 1953 [2008], §593, p. 131)

To avoid this philosophical disease, the approach adopted in this book was first to distinguish between collective action on the market and non-market collective action. We eliminated the first, whether illegal (cartels, conspiracies) or legal (strategic alliances). A cartel is a form of organized collective action (Dumez & Jeunemaître, 2000) but its object is limited. Similarly, for a strategic alliance between two companies. These forms of collective action seemed to us too far removed from the forms that developed in the nineteenth century and that prohibited direct effect on the market – chambers of commerce and trade associations (although some trade associations may have been condemned under the antitrust laws). So, we chose to focus on non-market collective action. We then sought to identify concrete supports and organizational devices. That is to say, along the lines of Ahrne and Brunsson (2008), we centered the analysis on, in their words, "decided orders," that is, organizations, and eliminating networks, which are "emergent orders" not decided ones (Chisholm, 1996). We arrived at the concept of FCADs. This allowed us to provide a synoptic view or a "perspicuous representation" of the phenomenon linking organizations that are not often linked to each other: chambers of commerce, trade associations, specialized meta-organizations, multistakeholder organizations. These FCADs are deployed at the local, national, supranational, sectoral, subsector, sectoral, and cross-sectoral levels; they may involve only companies, or companies and other actors (states, non-governmental organization [NGOs]). It seemed essential to report on this diversity in order to conduct better-founded analyses. The notion of heterarchy as we have redefined it allows us to explore this diversity, as well as a cost–benefit analysis of collective action in dynamics.

We sought to articulate this diversity with a historical approach. Surprisingly, at regular intervals, researchers are interested in collective action between firms as if it were new and as if it had been little studied. We cited, for example, Barnett's remark that "the lack of research on trade associations is lamentable" (Barnett, 2013, p. 214). In fact, the literature on trade associations is abundant and long-standing, as this book shows. What was missing was a synoptic view. In practice, the synoptic view and historical approach must be combined. Several important points then appear:

1. It appears that collective action between firms has always combined two prototypical devices – the chamber of commerce (cross-sectoral) and the trade association (sectoral). This means that managers need information both about what is happening in their sector and what is happening in other sectors that may be important to their particular business.
2. It also appears that these organizational forms are surprisingly stable. Many trade associations or chambers of commerce that were created in the late nineteenth century or early twentieth century still exist today.
3. Stable in nature, they have been able to adapt: the globalization of markets and industries has, for example, led to the creation of international trade sectoral associations and the International Chamber of Commerce (Fahey, 1921; Jimenez, 1996).
4. The portfolio of activities of these FCADs was determined as early as the 1920s and it also remained stable. For example, codes of ethics existed even then. The wave of corporate social responsibility (CSR) has probably boosted the activity of FCADs in this area, but it has not created it. Similarly, membership services already existed in the 1920s, although

some researchers believe that their appearance is more recent. On the other hand, it is rare for an FCAD to cover the entire portfolio. Each ensures a bundle or "bouquet" of activities of its own and that can evolve over time.

5. With regard to dynamics, McCormick (1996) is right: FCADs alternate phases of activity and phases of dormancy. We explained these alternations by the structure of the costs and benefits of collective action in dynamics. The direct costs (membership fees) are low compared to the turnover of firms, whether they are small and medium-sized enterprises (SMEs) or whether they are large companies. Therefore, removing an FCAD is not very compelling, especially since it can still be used in the future. On the other hand, the indirect costs, the active participation of managers in the activities of the FCAD, can be important. If the benefits of collective action are low, companies choose to reduce these indirect costs and the meta-organization becomes dormant. Determining that a meta-organization is active or dormant is not easy, neither for the actors involved nor for the researcher who studies it. When interviewed, actors who continue to participate in activities tend to emphasize the activity being conducted; actors who no longer participate are more skeptical of this activity.

6. What is also shown by the historical approach is that the two prototypical organizational forms are no longer the only ones to organize collective action between firms. We have seen the creation of specialized FCADs aiming to solve a certain type of problem and multistakeholder meta-organizations (Bastianutti & Dumez, 2018; Berkowitz, Bucheli & Dumez, 2017; Marques, 2017; Raymond & DeNardis, 2015). These new forms of FCADs have not replaced the two prototypical forms. On the contrary, they often rely on them or even include them (the Office Franco-Allemand pour la Transition Énergétique [OFATE], for example, has firms, NGOs, states, and trade associations as members; the United Nations Global Compact [UNGC] relies on trade associations to develop its Local Networks programs).

FUTURE DIRECTIONS

This book has laid the groundwork for an analysis of FCADs and business meta-organizations. Future research is needed to better illuminate the following:

1. The articulation between hierarchical and heterarchical dimensions in this type of device is central, as we have seen. The double kingpins, the president and the managing director (appointed), should be the subject of a comprehensive study. This is a relationship and it should be studied as such. The way it works largely determines the effectiveness of the action

of the meta-organization. The president enjoys the legitimacy of his or her election by the members. The managing director has the knowledge of the organization, experience in the role, and often long duration in his or her position (whereas the president exercises his or her function only for limited mandates). But we must also look at the rules of heterarchy and hierarchy, as well as at their articulation (our case study shows that the president has the monopoly on the negotiations with the public authorities). A comparative study of constitutions of business meta-organizations would be interesting. It might profitably mobilize the qualitative comparative analysis (QCA) method developed by Charles Ragin (Ragin, 1987, 2000; Kogut & Ragin, 2006).

2. It would also be interesting to work on the different families of FCADs, including multistakeholder meta-organizations, cross-sectoral meta-organizations, and specialized meta-organizations. There is also a need to look at how hierarchy and heterarchy are articulated differently in traditional business meta-organizations and in multistakeholder meta-organizations (Berkowitz et al., 2017). This should include understanding why companies in a sector choose to create a new meta-organization to address a particular problem, rather than creating a special committee within the trade association representing the sector.

3. In terms of dynamics, we should study more precisely how a business meta-organization becomes dormant – a "boring" organization in Ahrne and Brunsson's (2008) sense – and how it can be reawakened. This alternation of dormant and active phases raises the question of the maintenance of expertise and knowledge during these phases. In particular, the differences in distributed knowledge between dormancy and active phases should be studied.

4. Also with regard to dynamics, we notice splits at the sector level, with the creation of a new meta-organization, followed by phases of stabilization without new creation, sometimes (but rarely) with mergers. There are no systematic studies of these dynamics. The three phenomena – splits, stabilization phases, mergers – would need to be analyzed separately by comparing several sectors, and also in their succession over a long period at the sector level. More generally, we should be able to study the joint dynamics of the sectors and meta-organizations that represent them. In our case study, we see, for example, that the sequence – birth of a sector, creation of a meta-organization that represents this sector, lobbying to obtain from the state a regulatory framework favorable to the development of the sector – is not relevant. The sector, the organization that represents it (or rather makes it exist as a sector) and public policy in favor of the sector appeared at the same time. Dynamically, it is necessary to study the sectors, the devices that organize collective action of the companies of the

sector, and the public policies having an impact on the sectors at the same time. The business history could then shed important light on the interactions between these three dimensions.

5. We constructed a dynamic cost–benefit model of collective action, based on the distinction between direct and indirect costs on the one hand and collective and individual benefits on the other. This model needs to be tested by quantitative studies. Case studies could then show the relevance of this model and confirm the division of the dynamics of meta-organizations into temporal nodes.

6. The blind spot of the study of FCADs is the assessment of their impact on society and the economy as a whole on welfare. Olson opened up this field of study with his book published in 1982, but his conclusions do not appear solid. Recognition that these organizations may be active or dormant, and that it is difficult to distinguish between these phases of action and dormancy, greatly complicates the assessment of their impact. Today, however, there are econometric methods that should make it possible to reopen this assessment.

7. One last question should be asked: can social networks today profoundly change the activity of business meta-organizations? As we have seen, for reasons of cost, advertising campaigns being very expensive, FCADs have rarely sought to intervene directly on the general public. Their activity has focused more on political subsystems. Social networks can suddenly threaten firms in a sector and destabilize them. In response, trade associations and other FCADs can intervene on social networks and thus more directly on the general public, even if the word of the lobbies is always suspect.

Much research remains to be done to understand the functioning, the role, and the impact of collective action schemes created by companies or in which they participate, but we hope to have laid the foundations for these analyses in this book.

Appendix: methodologies

Studying the way in which firms organize themselves collectively poses a series of methodological problems, which we began to discuss in previous chapters. The first is the understanding of the diversity of the forms of devices used, the trade association being only one of these forms among many. This diversity makes the census of these devices very difficult and always imperfect. Longitudinal (historical) studies are also difficult because of the often very long life of these devices (several decades). Having access to their operation, knowing that these devices often practice lobbying, is also not easy. Finally, assessing the political and economic impact of these devices is also difficult. At regular intervals, researchers point out the theoretical and practical issues of studying this political, economic, and social phenomenon, which undoubtedly plays an important role in the dynamics of our societies (Lawton, Rajwani & Minto, 2018). The methodologies used are multiple, each with their own benefits and limitations. This appendix attempts to highlight these problems.

TO APPREHEND THE DIVERSITY OF FIRMS' COLLECTIVE ACTION DEVICES (FCADS)

The devices used by companies to act collectively appear very different: there are chambers of commerce, trade associations, trade associations specialized in a type of problem (the environment, for example), clubs bringing together companies from various sectors (Potoski & Prakash, 2005; Prakash & Potoski, 2007), and so on. When we face a class of empirical objects like this, we usually try to find a concept, that is, we search for a definition that captures the core that is common to each:

> [M]uch work in philosophy, psychology, linguistics, and anthropology assumes that categories are logical bounded entities, membership in which is defined by an item's possession of a simple set of criterial features, in which all instances possessing the criterial attributes have a full and equal degree of membership. (Rosch & Mervis, 1975, pp. 573–4)

Inspired by Wittgenstein (1953 [2008]), however, another approach has developed, based on the concept that categories are made up of prototype and non-prototype members. For example, in the furniture category, a chair, not a radio, is a prototype (Ginzburg, 2004; Rosch, 1978; Rosch & Mervis, 1975). This is based on Wittgenstein's notion of family resemblance:

> A family resemblance relationship consists of a set of items of the form AB, BC, CD, DE. That is, each item has at least one, and probably several, elements in common with one or more other items, but no, or few, elements are common to all items. (Rosch & Mervis, 1975, p. 575)

As an example, this approach has been used to address the empirical diversity of phenomena covered by the word "market" (Depeyre & Dumez, 2008).

When examining the devices used by firms to organize collectively, no common definition appears. On the other hand, family resemblances emerge from three possible choices: sectoral, non-sectoral, and geographical (and institutional level). As far as the sector is concerned, there is, of course, a prototype that is the trade association. Note that this can be local, national, or supranational (at European level, for example, or worldwide). Note also that the notion of sector is still vague – as previously stated, Naylor (1921) already explained that the American Paper and Pulp Association represented the entire American paper industry but that there were also associations representing subsectors such as the Tissue Paper Manufacturers' Association. But, we saw that we could find in the same sector devices that move away from the prototype. We thus find meta-organizations grouping the firms of the same sector but specialized in the search for a solution to a problem posed to the sector (environmental, for example). We are still referring to the sector, but specializing in a problem, which is not the case for the trade association. A number of clubs can also be found at sector level – a few companies in the sector group together to launch an initiative that widens the gap with other companies in the sector (Potoski & Prakash, 2005; Prakash & Potoski, 2007). This strategy may be stable or transitory. Either the club remains definitively closed (which a trade association is not) with a strategy of "fencing out the Jones's"; or, it opens the second time to all the companies of the sector – "teaming up the Jones's" – like the Cement Sustainability Initiative (Bastianutti & Dumez, 2018). So, in reference to the sector, we can identify a family of devices that can be quite removed from the prototype of the trade association.

Historically, the prototype of the non-sectoral collective action device is the chamber of commerce (Bennett, 2011). Again, this device can be local, regional, national, or even supranational (the International Chamber of Commerce [ICC], whose slogan is "We Are the World Business Organization"). But, the family also includes clubs that bring together companies from different sectors to solve a societal problem. They can also be at a local level (a business club that tries to solve a health problem, such as curbing the AIDS epidemic in a region) or at a global level (such as the World Business Council for

Sustainable Development [WBCSD] that brings together 200 companies worldwide).

As seen in the first two families, the geographical and institutional level chosen may be local, regional, national, or supranational. At the local level, chambers of commerce and industry and trade associations can be found. You can also find clubs with various goals. It is the same at the world level where there are trade associations such as the Global Cement Industry Association and its partner the WBCSD (some cement companies are members but it includes firms from various sectors).

Table A.1   Empirical diversity of firms' collective action devices

Meta-organizations	Local	National	Supranational
Sectoral level			
Non-specialized	Eastern Kansas Oil & Gas Association	Portland Cement Association, US)	Global Cement Industry Association
Specialized			Cement Sustainability Initiative
Cross-sectoral level			
Non-specialized	Liverpool Chamber of Commerce & Industry	The British Chambers of Commerce	International Chamber of Commerce
Specialized		Les Entreprises pour la Cité (French firms teaming up on issues of corporate social responsibility)	Global Business Initiative (advancing corporate respect for human rights)
Multistakeholder	Health Alliance in Guangdong (China)	Global Compact local networks	United Nations Global Compact

Table A.1 gives examples of the diverse forms of FCADs (see above). This table brings order to the empirical diversity of collective action schemes put in place by firms, but it does not completely cover it for at least two reasons. As we have seen, there are also subsectoral and supra-sectoral systems. On the other hand, the sector should not be considered as a closed entity with well-defined borders – the sectors overlap. Many firms are diversified, so they belong to several sectors. It is therefore necessary to reason in terms of family resemblance and this is how the table should be read.

For sets of a few dozen meta-organizations – for example, if a sectoral rather than a national approach is adopted (see below) – another approach to diversity might be possible: qualitative comparative analysis (QCA), developed by Charles Ragin (1987, 2000). This approach makes it possible to examine diversity when it is limited to about four to 50 cases and does not lend itself to statistical analysis (Kogut & Ragin, 2006). To our knowledge, this methodology has not yet been used to analyze FCADs.

THE DIFFICULTY IN QUANTIFYING FIRMS' COLLECTIVE ACTION DEVICES

At the national level, there are directories listing business meta-organizations. For example, in the US, one can find them registered in *The Encyclopedia of Associations: National Organizations of the U.S.* (Atterberry, 2013). But then you have to do a sorting job and make choices. For example, Spillman sorted them on the following basis:

> The population census includes those nonprofit associations composed of members drawn from more than one locality or state who share a common orientation to some sector or industry, trade, business, or commercial activities. (Spillman, 2012, p. 14)

The result gives a population of 4465 national business associations in 2012 in the US. From central business directory research and other sources, similarly, Bennett (1998) tried to identify trade associations in the UK. He arrived at a total of about 3000. The comparison of Spillman's calculation for the US and Bennett's for the UK raises questions: given the relative size of the US economy and the UK economy, it seems that business organizations are proportionally more numerous in the UK than in the US. In fact, Spillman and Bennett take into account trade associations, that is, meta-organizations in the strict sense (organizations whose members are companies), which account for 56 percent of the total, and professional associations (whose members are individuals), accounting for 44 percent of the total. But Bennett adds chambers of commerce, organizations whose members can be organizations or sole proprietorships, that bring together all economic sectors at the local level. Since Spillman excludes representative business organizations operating only at the level of a locality or a state, this *de facto* excludes chambers of commerce. We cannot therefore make a rigorous comparison between the US and the UK on the basis of Spillman's and Bennett's figures. In any case, rather than precise figures, these are only indicative (Bennett, 1998, p. 1377). On the other hand, a national approach excludes international meta-organizations, which play a role that can be considered important in the problems of globalization (human rights, environmental, sustainable development).

Berkowitz, Bucheli and Dumez (2017) did not adopt entry by country (USA, UK, France, Germany, etc.) but entry by sector, and tried to list the business meta-organizations in the oil and gas industry. The constructed database contains 93 items. But again, these are only indicative figures. One can indeed identify national trade associations (almost every country belonging to the

UN has a national trade association of oil and gas companies operating on its territory), but in the US, for example, there are also trade associations at the state level (Colorado Oil & Gas Association, Eastern Kansas Oil & Gas Association, Illinois Oil & Gas Association, etc.). These have not been entered in the database.

The study of the phenomenon at the sector level also shows the complexity of counting due to fuzzy boundaries between sectors. It is necessary to consider the subsectoral, sectoral, supra-sectoral and cross-sectoral levels. The oil and gas industry is in fact divided into subsectors and there are meta-organizations for the upstream, the midstream, and the downstream organizations (for example, in the UK, the UK Petroleum Industry Association represents companies of the whole industry, and the UK Offshore Operators Association represents the offshore sector alone; Boleat, 1996, p. 13). Supra-sectoral concerns areas for which oil companies face the same problems as firms in other sectors and have formed common meta-organizations. For example, oil and gas companies are found in the supra-sector of extractive industries with mining companies; offshore oil exploitation is found with fisheries and shipping in the supra-sector of marine industries; but oil companies (Chevron, Total) can find themselves with companies from completely different sectors (Siemens, Hewlett Packard, Hilton) in cross-sectoral meta-organizations like the Global Business Initiative on Human Rights. Finally, many oil companies operate within the chemistry field and are members of trade associations in this sector. This last phenomenon has not been considered in Berkowitz et al.'s (2017) constructed database. In practice, because of the unclear boundaries between sectors and the fact that large companies belong to several segments of a sector and to several sectors, the meta-organization count at the level of a sector appears problematic and it only gives an indication. Interviews with a petroleum firm have shown that the firm itself has difficulty quantifying the number of meta-organizations to which it belongs.

An accurate quantification of meta-organizations at the state level, as at the sectoral level, is therefore difficult to achieve. Moreover, in the oil and gas industry, the study conducted did not show any cases of disappearance, only cases of name change of meta-organization or fusion between meta-organizations. Bennett's study in the UK shows an important stability with an average lifespan of 45 years, but notes changes in the population. Bennett estimates these changes at 1 percent per year – disappearance, name change, merger of two meta-organizations – the renewal rate of companies being 6.3 percent per year: "they are much more stable than the businesses they represent" (Bennett, 1998, p. 1385). Despite this stability, not only are the figures inaccurate, but they are constantly changing, albeit at a rate of 1 percent per year. On the other hand, the trends are quite clear: the meta-organizations are mechanisms of collective action between firms that appeared with the development of companies, and especially large companies, at the end of the nineteenth century (see Chapter 2), devices that are still used today. Since their appearance, they are multiple, with different approaches: the trade associations represent the firms of the same sector and the chambers of commerce represent firms belonging to very different sectors but facing common problems at the local level (Bennett, 1996). It is as if the firms faced common problems on different levels – sectors, subsectors, close sectors, at local, regional, national, supranational levels – and that they each adapted the collective action device to the nature of the problem, knowing that, problems being multiple, these devices are also multiple. A complementary factor, which was mentioned by a CEO during an interview in the cement industry, is that business leaders are constantly faced with the need to collect and decipher weak signals that characterize the environment of the company. Participation in collective action devices belonging to different families (specific to their sector, local, global, with other sectors, with partners other than companies, etc.) allows them to better cover the complexity of the problem in the business environment, and thus better identify risks and opportunities (Grove, 1996).

LONGITUDINAL STUDIES

A longitudinal study consists of following the long-term dynamics of an organization (Bucheli & Wadhwani, 2014; Pettigrew, 1990). There are quite a few longitudinal studies of business meta-organizations over a very long period. One of the rare examples is Lynn McCormick's PhD dissertation on the Tooling and Manufacturing Association created in the mid-1920s as a trade association of the Chicago metalworking industry (McCormick, 1996). The author analyzes over 70 years of this trade association. The literature is divided (see previous chapter) between those who emphasize the weakness of collective action between firms (conflicts, slowness, or inability to reach consensus and action, chronic lack of means) and those who emphasize the effectiveness of this collective action (ability to create rents of influence through lobbying, ability to manage information, ability to improve the productivity of members through the provision of adapted services). Thanks to her study over the long term, Lynn McCormick brings an original and new vision. She highlights a lifecycle with phases of success (high returns, greater bargaining power, and high performance for the industry) and phases of decline. Despite its interest, McCormick's study shows the difficulties of longitudinal research. It can only rely on archives. These only begin once the meta-organization is created. To know under what circumstances this creation took place it would be necessary to interview the actors who created it. But, if it goes back more than 50 years, the researcher is no longer able to draw from the interviews of those behind the creation of the trade association, as Naylor had already noted:

> There has been no uniformity in the initial causes of the organization of the older trade associations. Like "Topsy," a great many of them just grew, and the rest found their beginnings under circumstances so nebulous and indefinite that the direct reason or source of their origin is not obtainable. (Naylor, 1921, p. 39)

If the researcher selects a trade association of too recent creation, he or she can interview the actors who created it, but he or she cannot lead a satisfactory study of the dynamics of this meta-organization, the passage of time being insufficient.

In addition, McCormick's study has the advantage of attempting to account both for the dynamics of the sector and the dynamics of the meta-organization that represents it, in their interactions, over a period of 70 years. Thus, the study of the meta-organization itself, in the dynamics of its operation, is not thorough and the reader does not know how the meta-organization "represented" the sector.

THE INNER WORKINGS OF FIRMS' COLLECTIVE ACTION DEVICES

To study a business meta-organization, an approach by studying its visible production is possible. This approach is adopted by Spillman (2012). She studied a representative sample of 25 American trade associations (hence meta-organizations; Spillman, 2018). She collected all the documents produced and posted on the websites. An enormous amount of data was generated: trawled systematically, these websites each included a minimum of about 20 to more than 500 pages, with more in the upper range. More than 30 sorts of "documents" were available, in many different forms. They included, for example, statements of purpose, committee reports, membership criteria, by-laws, strategic plans, "state-of-the-industry" analyses and prognoses, elaborate technical information, industry and association histories, awards, meeting agendas and convention programs, records of past meetings, archives of newsletters, directories of members, accreditation procedures and standards, information about scholarship and charity programs, safety guides, and promotional information. A surprisingly large proportion of this discourse was oriented to the knowledgeable in-group audience, mostly to the members, rather than to publics or markets (moreover, sites generally displayed few images that might engage outsiders; Spillman, 2012, pp. 14–15).

The aim was to understand how businesspeople make sense of their action, to understand how trade associations create solidarity in collective identity. Therefore, the vision that the capitalist economic action is based on self-interested action is challenged and business associations appear in a new light – they are not simply organizational tools for the promotion of business interests (Spillman, 2012, p. 20). On the other hand, Spillman's approach does not make it possible to understand the inner workings of business meta-organizations, the concrete way in which collective action is built and whose solidarity may or may not appear in the context of this collective action. Galambos (1966) mainly worked on archives, including businesspeople's letters. They show the difficulty of collective action (standardization, the attempt to control production and prices in a sector made up of small firms). Lynn and McKeown (1988) conducted interviews in both the US and Japan, but they had no real access to the inner workings of the trade associations they studied. Naylor, who had personal experience of working in a trade association, did not speak directly of this experience, but, as we saw in Chapter 2, he gives details of the concrete difficulties of collective action within this type of organization.

THE DIFFICULTIES OF ASSESSMENT

As seen earlier, evaluating the role of collective action schemes created by companies also poses difficult methodological problems, both at the macroeconomic level and at the sectoral level. Olson (1982) has been widely criticized for the lack of rigor in his demonstration of his macroeconomic thesis, that is, that the stability of collective action structures leads to a decline in the dynamism of economies. The study conducted by Lynn and McKeown (1988) of trade associations in Japan shows that the dynamism of the Japanese economy after 1945 is certainly not due, at least mainly, to the disappearance of these structures that have changed their name, or functions, but which remained finally quite stable.

The opposite thesis – that trade associations and other business meta-organizations could boost the economy – is not demonstrated either. In fact, there are indications that trade associations embrace economic cycles in their dynamics. For example, during the crisis of the early 1980s, 32 percent of American trade associations experienced a drop in staff numbers (Lynn & McKeown, 1988). It might be thought that during the growth phases of the economy, trade associations also grow, and that they tend to shrink in periods of crisis (companies seeking to save money and being reluctant during these periods to assume membership costs). The idea that, according to their mode of operation, business meta-organizations can have a beneficial effect on the economy in general or, on the contrary, a negative effect, appears reasonable. But to show rigorously under what conditions these positive or negative effects are triggered is difficult. For the moment anyway, empirical evidence is lacking.

The same is true at the sectoral level. Laumann and Knoke (1987, 1988) present two of the few in-depth studies of how the relationship between a sector and the state occurs. Their studies show, as we have seen, a balkanized state facing in a rather haphazard manner a multitude of more or less organized sectors and pressure groups. There is no general rule and no possible comprehensive vision: a well-organized sector around a trade association can efficiently obtain a regulatory and incentive framework to ensure favorable conditions for its development or block measures that would be unfavorable; a less well-organized sector, facing powerful non-governmental organizations around a topic that mobilizes them, can get much less. To this vision of a sort of disorder that is difficult to evaluate, McCormick (1996) adds, as we have seen, the idea of cycles. A trade association can be particularly effective in its negotiations with the state at certain times and dormant at others.

THE ADOPTED APPROACH

To study the functioning of trade associations and other business meta-organizations, the case study appears the most appropriate methodology (Dumez, 2015; Eisenhardt, 1989; Yin, 2003). The limit is obviously the uniqueness of the studied case, which cannot lend itself to any generalization of a statistical type but can nevertheless allow an analytical generalization (Yin, 2003).

Our selected case study is that of the emergence of the renewable energy (RE) sector in France. It has a number of interesting features. It emerged in the 1990s. The study period (more than 25 years) allows us a sufficient perspective to analyze the dynamics of the sector while not being too long, thus enabling the interview of actors who were at the origin of the emergence. In addition, the case has "extreme" characteristics in of Seawright and Gerring's (2008) sense. First, the emergence of this sector was unlikely. Politically, France made the choice in the 1970s to invest heavily in nuclear energy. Economically, the system produces cheap electricity that makes the emergence of substitutes very difficult. In terms of climate and the environment, nuclear produces little greenhouse gas. The political and economic obstacles to the emergence of an RE sector thus appeared to be damaging. Moreover, it is difficult to speak of a "sector." Indeed, the term "renewable energies" covers very different economic activities (land and sea wind, anaerobic digestion, solar thermal and photovoltaic, hydroelectric, geothermal, etc.) because of the size of the actors involved, the technologies used, the dynamics of development (some face problems of acceptability, others do not). It is the negotiations between the state and the renewable energies association, the trade association created by the actors that created the sector and maintained its existence.

This trade association is the Syndicat des Énergies Renouvelables (Trade Association of Renewable Energies – SER). There are also subsector trade associations, in wind energy (FEE) or in photovoltaics (ENERPLAN), but the SER represents the entire RE sector (it was created in 1993 as the SIPROFER and became the SER in 1998). There are currently 14 members of staff, which makes it a fairly big meta-organization even internationally.[1]

The research material comprises secondary data, especially institutional communications, that is, information produced by organizations themselves (the same kind of data that Spillman collected). Nevertheless, their "association" status exempts them from communicating their balance sheet. The information provided by these data has therefore proved to be rather limited. These data have also been triangulated with other reports from the French Agence de l'Environnement et de la Maîtrise de l'Énergie (Public Environment and Energy Management Agency – ADEME), the Ministry of the Environment, as well as with public or specialized press articles.

The collection of primary data about our case was carried out through interviews whose goals were: (1) to obtain a historical view of the whole period of existence of the industry and the related meta-organization(s) since its creation; and (2) to test the ideas of researchers on the role of meta-organizations (Piore, 2006). We conducted a dozen interviews with former presidents or managers of the RE meta-organizations in France. Most of them are entrepreneurs (in RE or other industries) besides their activity at the collective level. The interviews were non-directive: we explained to the interviewees that our research program was on collective action in the industry, and let them speak about the way it developed, how it worked, and what kind of role the trade association played. In parallel with the interviews, secondary data were studied – mainly official reports, articles in specialized journals, and press articles. Two researchers independently coded these data.

The case study approach provides access to one of the central activities of this type of organization – collective lobbying. This is indirect access, through retrospective interviews, but lobbying is hardly observable by a researcher and it is probably the only possible access in practice. By interviewing actors from meta-organizations, journalists, and government officials, it is possible to understand at least part of the way in which this activity is carried out.

CONCLUSION

The study of firms' collective action devices poses difficult methodological problems. First, it is difficult to know where to place the empirical limits of the object to be studied – some studies look only at the national trade associations (meta-organizations), others add the professional associations (whose members are individuals), some exclude chambers of commerce, others include them, some study the phenomenon only at the national level, others study it only at the international level without the connection being made between the two levels. In total, the figures are therefore very fluctuating. While these mechanisms may be thought to play an important role in the dynamics of contemporary economies, this role is difficult to assess at the macro-, meso- or microeconomic levels.

Several types of problem make the study of FCADs difficult to conduct. One must explore their diversity, knowing that they can be found at the sector level (trade associations, but also meta-organizations specialized in the resolution of a particular problem), at the subsectoral level, at the intersectoral level, at the cross-sectoral level, and that there are also multistakeholder meta-organizations. If this diversity is complicated to understand, the quantification of the phenomenon is also hard to conduct and can vary in considerable proportions. The longitudinal approach is rendered difficult by the often very long life of this type of organization. To the extent, finally, where one of the main activities of these devices is lobbying, it is not easy to gain access to their operation and their activities and the evaluation of the impact of these activities is not easy. In addition to an analysis of the literature on this type of organization, which has not so far been fully explored in its various dimensions, we chose to study a sector: (1) whose existence depended on the policies led by the state, that of renewable energies (in the French case where successive governments have made the political choice of nuclear, so were *a priori* rather hostile to renewable energies); (2) that is old enough to allow a longitudinal study (it appeared in the 1990s); while (3) being recent enough to allow us to meet the actors who were there at its birth.

NOTE

1. In the United States, only 23 percent of trade associations have a staff of more than 12 people (Spillman, 2012).

References

Abbott, A. (1995), "Things of boundaries," *Social Research*, **62**(4), 857–82.

Abegglen, J. (ed.) (1970), *Business Strategies for Japan*, Tokyo: Sophia University Press.

Ahrne, G. & N. Brunsson (2005), "Organizations and meta-organizations," *Scandinavian Journal of Management*, **21**(4), 429–49.

Ahrne, G. & N. Brunsson (2008), *Meta-organizations*, Cheltenham, UK and Northampton, MA, USA: Edward Elgar Publishing.

Ahrne, G. & N. Brunsson (2011), "Organization outside organizations: the significance of partial organization," *Organization*, **18**(1), 83–104.

Ahuja, G. & S. Yayavaram (2011), "Explaining influence rents: the case for an institutions-based view of strategy," *Organization Science*, **22**(6), 1631–52.

Aldrich, H.E. (2018), "Trade associations matter as units of selection, as actors within comparative and historical institutional frameworks, and as potential impediments to societal wide collective action," *Journal of Management Inquiry*, **27**(1), 21–5.

Aldrich, H.E. & U. Staber (1988), "Organizing business interests: patterns of trade association foundings, transformations, and deaths," in G.R. Carroll (ed.), *Ecological Models of Organization*, Cambridge, MA: Ballinger, pp. 111–26.

Aldrich, H., C. Zimmer, U. Staber & J. Beggs (1994), "Minimalism, mutualism, and maturity: the evolution of the American trade association population in the 20th century," in J. Baum & J. Singh (eds), *Evolutionary Dynamics of Organization*, New York: Oxford University Press, pp. 223–39.

Alexander, J. (2006), *The Civil Sphere*, Oxford: Oxford University Press.

Arendt, H. (1961), *Between Past and Future: Eight Exercises in Political Science*, New York: The Viking Press.

Astley, W.G. & C. Fombrun (1983), "Collective strategy: social ecology of organizational environments," *Academy of Management Review*, **8**(4), 576–87.

Atterberry, T.E. (2013), *Encyclopedia of Associations: National Organizations of the U.S.* (52nd edition), Farmington Hills, MI: Gale.

Baines, P.R. & H. Viney (2010), "The unloved relationship? Dynamic capabilities and political-market strategy: a research agenda," *Journal of Public Affairs*, **10**(4), 258–64.

Bang, P.F. (2008), *The Roman Bazaar: A Comparative Study of Trade and Markets in a Tributary Empire*, New York: Cambridge University Press.

Barnett, M.L. (2013), "One voice, but whose voice? Exploring what drives trade association activity," *Business & Society*, **52**(2), 213–44.

Barnett, M.L. (2018), "Beyond the membership decision: how do trade associations manage firm involvement?" *Journal of Management Inquiry*, **27**(1), 10–12.

Barnett, M.L. and A.A. King (2008), "Good fences make good neighbors: a longitudinal analysis of an industry self-regulatory institution," *Academy of Management Journal*, **5**(6), 1150–70.

Baron, D.P. (2006), *Business and its Environment* (5th edition), Upper Saddle River, NJ: Prentice Hall.

Baron, D.P. (2016), "Strategy beyond markets: a step back and a look forward," in J.M. De Figueiredo, M. Lenox, F. Oberholzer-Gee & R.G. Vanden Bergh (eds), *Strategy Beyond Markets (Advances in Strategic Management, Volume 34)*, Bingley, UK: Emerald Group Publishing, pp. 1–54.

Bastianutti, J. & H. Dumez (2012), "Pourquoi les entreprises sont-elles désormais reconnues comme socialement responsables?" [Why are companies now recognized as socially responsible?], *Gérer et Comprendre*, No. 109, 44–54.

Bastianutti, J. & H. Dumez (2018), "Environmental sustainability for industry legitimacy and competitiveness: the case of CSR collective strategies in the cement industry," in H. Borland, A. Lindgreen & J. Vanhamme et al. (eds), *Business Strategies for Sustainability: A Research Anthology*, Abingdon, UK and New York: Routledge, pp. 385–400.

Batelle Memorial Institute (1956), *Research by Cooperative Organizations: A Survey of Scientific Research by Trade Associations, Professional and Technical Societies, and Other Cooperative Groups. Prepared for the National Science Foundation*, Washington, DC: Government Printing Office.

Baumgartner, F.R. & B.D. Jones (1991), "Agenda dynamics and policy subsystems," *The Journal of Politics*, **53**(4), 1044–74.

Becker, H.S. (1995), "Moral entrepreneurs: the creation and enforcement of deviant categories," in N.J. Herman (ed.), *Deviance: A Symbolic Interactionist Approach*, New York: General Hall, pp. 169–78.

Bennett, R.J. (1995), "The logic of local business associations: the analysis of voluntary chambers of commerce," *Journal of Public Policy*, **15**(3), 251–79.

Bennett, R.J. (1996), "Can transaction cost economies explain voluntary chambers of commerce?" *Journal of Institutional and Theoretical Economics*, **152**(4), 653–80.

Bennett, R.J. (1998), "Business associations and their potential to contribute to economic development: reexploring an interface between the state and market," *Environment and Planning*, **30**(8), 1367–87.

Bennett, R.J. (2000), "The logic of membership of sectoral associations," *Review of Social Economy*, **58**(1), 17–42.

Bennett, R.J. (2011), *Local Business Voice: The History of Chambers of Commerce in Britain, Ireland, and Revolutionary America, 1760–2011*, Oxford: Oxford University Press.

Berkowitz, H., M. Bucheli & H. Dumez (2017), "Collectively designing CSR through meta-organizations: a case study of the oil and gas industry," *Journal of Business Ethics*, **143**(4), 753–69.

Berkowitz, H. & H. Dumez (2015), "La dynamique des dispositifs d'action collective entre firmes: le cas des métaorganisations dans le secteur pétrolier" [The dynamics of collective action devices between firms: the case of meta-organizations in the petroleum sector], *L'Année Sociologique*, **65**(2), 333–56.

Berkowitz, H. & H. Dumez (2016), "The concept of meta-organization: issues for management studies," *European Management Review*, **13**(2), 149–56.

Berry, J.M. & C. Wilcox (2018), *The Interest Group Society* (6th edition), Abingdon, UK and New York: Routledge.

Boleat, M. (1996), *Trade Association Strategy and Management*, London: Association of British Insurers.

Bonardi, J.-P. (2008), "The internal limits to firms' nonmarket strategies," *The European Management Review*, **5**(3), 165–74.

Bonardi, J.-P., G.L.F. Holburn & R.G. Vanden Bergh (2006), "Nonmarket strategy in regulated industries: theory and evidence from U.S. electric utilities," *Academy of Management Journal*, **49**(6), 1209–28.

Bonardi, J.-P. & R.G. Vanden Bergh (2015), "Political knowledge and the resource-based view," in T.C. Lawton & T.S. Rajwani (eds) (2015), *The Routledge Companion to Non-Market Strategy*, Abingdon, UK and New York: Routledge, pp. 12–28.

Brandenburger, A.M. & B.J. Nalebuff (1996), *Coopetition*, New York: Doubleday.

Brunsson, N. (2003), *The Organization of Hypocrisy: Talk, Decisions and Actions in Organizations*, Copenhagen: Copenhagen Business School Press.

Buchanan, S. (2016), "Trade associations and the strategic framing of change in contested issue organizational fields: the evolution of sustainability in the Canadian mining industry (1993–2013)," PhD dissertation, Schulich School of Business, Canada.

Bucheli, M. & R.D. Wadhwani (eds) (2014), *Organizations in Time: History, Theory, Methods*, Oxford: Oxford University Press.

Büthe, T. & W. Mattli (2011), *The New Global Rulers: The Privatization of Regulation in the World Economy*, Princeton, NJ: Princeton University Press.

Cartel, M., E. Boxenbaum & F. Aggeri (2019), "Just for fun!: How experimental spaces stimulate innovation in institutionalized fields," *Organization Studies*, **40**(1), 65–92.

Cartwright, T.J. (1987), "The lost art of planning," *Long Range Planning*, **20**(2), 92–9.

Chisholm, R.F. (1996), "On the meaning of networks," *Group & Organization Management*, **21**(2), 216–35.

Coleman, W.D. (1985), "Analysing the associative action of business: policy advocacy and policy participation," *Canadian Public Administration*, **28**(3), 413–33.

Conniff, J. (1975), "On the obsolescence of general will: Rousseau, Madison and the evolution of republican political thought," *Western Political Quarterly*, **28**, 47–58.

Crumley, C.L. (1979), "Three locational models: an epistemological assessment for anthropology and archaeology," in M.B. Schiffer (ed.), *Advances in Archaeological Method and Theory*, Amsterdam: Elsevier, pp. 141–73.

Crumley, C.L. (1995), "Heterarchy and the analysis of complex societies," *Archeological Papers of the American Anthropological Association*, **6**(1), 1–5.

Crumley, C.L. (2005), "Remember how to organize: heterarchy across disciplines," in W.W. Baden (ed.), *Nonlinear Models for Archaeology and Anthropology*, Abingdon, UK and New York: Routledge, pp. 35–50.

Dahl, R.A. (1956), *A Preface to Democratic Theory*, Chicago, IL: University of Chicago Press.

Debourdeau, A. (2011), "De la 'solution' au 'problème': la problématisation de l'obligation d'achat de l'énergie solaire photovoltaïque en France et en Allemagne" [From the "solution" to the "problem": the problematization of the obligation to purchase photovoltaic solar energy in France and Germany], *Politix*, **3**(95), 103–27.

De Landa, M. (1997), *A Thousand Years of Non-Linear History*, New York: Zone Books.

Dentoni, D. & V. Bitzer (2015), "The role(s) of universities in dealing with global wicked problems through multi-stakeholder initiatives," *Journal of Cleaner Production*, **106**, 68–78.

Dentoni, D., V. Bitzer & G. Schouten (2018), "Harnessing wicked problems in multi-stakeholder partnerships," *Journal of Business Ethics*, **150**(2), 333–56.

Depeyre, C. & H. Dumez (2008), "What is a market? A Wittgensteinian exercise," *European Management Review*, **5**(4), 225–31.

Djelic, M.-L. & F. den Hond (2014), "Introduction: multiplicity and plurality in the world of standards," *Business and Politics*, **16**(1), 67–77.

Doner, R.F. & B.R. Schneider (2000), "Business associations and economic development: why some associations contribute more than others," *Business and Politics*, **2**(3), 261–88.

Doran, G.T. (1981), "There's a S.M.A.R.T. way to write management goals and objectives," *Management Review*, **70**(11), 35–6.

Dorobantu, S., A. Kaul & B. Zelner (2017), "Nonmarket strategy research through the lens of new institutional economics: an integrative review and future directions," *Strategic Management Journal*, **38**(1), 114–40.

Dumez, H. (2012), "L'hypocrisie organisationnelle" [Organizational hypocrisy], in J.-M. Saussois (ed.), *Les organisations: état des savoirs*, Paris: Éditions Sciences Humaines, pp. 255–61.

Dumez, H. (2015), "What is a case, and what is a case study?" *Bulletin de Méthodologie Sociologique/Bulletin of Sociological Methodology*, No. 127, 43–57.

Dumez, H. & A. Jeunemaître (1989), *Diriger l'économie: l'État et les prix en France 1936-1986* [Leading the Economy: The State and Prices in France 1936–1986], Paris: L'Harmattan.

Dumez, H. & A. Jeunemaître (2000), *Understanding and Regulating the Market at a Time of Globalization: The Case of the Cement Industry*, Basingstoke: Palgrave Macmillan.

Dumez, H. & S. Renou (2018), "Les énergies renouvelables existent-elles et peut-on piloter la transition énergétique?" [Do renewable sources of energy exist? Can the energy transition be steered?], *Gérer et Comprendre*, No. 134, 3–13, accessed at http://www.annales.org/gc/GC-english-language-online-edition/2019/G&C19_4DumezRenou.pdf.

Eisenhardt, K.M. (1989), "Building theories from case study research," *Academy of Management Review*, **14**(4), 532–50.

Ellis, J.J. (2000), *Founding Brothers: The Revolutionary Generation*, New York: Alfred A. Knopf.

Elster, J. (1998), "A plea for mechanisms," in P. Hedstrøm & R. Swedberg (eds), *Social Mechanisms: An Analytical Approach to Social Theory*, Cambridge, UK: Cambridge University Press, pp. 45–73.

Epstein, S.A. (1991), *Wage, Labor and Guilds in Medieval Europe*, Chapel Hill, NC: University of North Carolina Press.

European Commission (2008), *Directive 2008/56/EC of the European Parliament and of the Council of 17 June 2008 Establishing a Framework for Community Action in the Field of Marine Environmental Policy*, accessed 22 March 2020 at https://eur-lex.europa.eu/legal-content/EN/TXT/?uri=CELEX%3A32008L0056.

Fahey, J.H. (1921), "The International Chamber of Commerce," *The Annals of the American Academy of Political and Social Science*, **94**, 126–30.

Foreville, R. (1985), "Du Domesday Book à la Grande Charte: guildes, franchises et chartes urbaines" [From the Domesday Book to the Magna Carta: guilds, franchises and urban charters], in *Actes des congrès de la société des historiens médiévistes de l'enseignement supérieur public*, 16ᵉ congrès Rouen, 1985, Lyon: Persée, pp. 163–74.

Foucault, M. (1980), *Power/Knowledge*, New York: Pantheon Books.

Fransen, L. (2012), "Multi-stakeholder governance and voluntary programme interactions: legitimation politics in the institutional design of corporate social responsibility," *Socio-Economic Review*, **10**(1), 163–92.

Frederick, W.C. & M.S. Myers (1983), "Public policy advertising and the 1980 presidential election," in L.E. Preston (ed.), *Research in Corporate Social Performance and Policy (Volume 5)*, Stamford, CT: JAI Press, pp. 56–89.

Freeman, J.B. (2018), *Behemoth: A History of the Factory and the Making of the Modern World*, New York: W.W. Norton & Company.

Fujii, M. (1948), "The Portland cement industry in Japan," *Pit & Quarry*, July, 103–9.

Fuller, L.L. (1968), *The Anatomy of Law*, Gretna, LA: Pelican Publishing.

Galambos, L. (1966), *Competition and Cooperation: The Emergence of a National Trade Association*, Baltimore, MD: Johns Hopkins University Press.

Galbraith, J.K. (1952), *A Theory of Price Control*, Cambridge, MA: Harvard University Press.

Ginzburg, C. (2004), "Family resemblances and family trees: two cognitive metaphors," *Critical Inquiry*, **30**, 537–56.

Girard, M. & D. Stark (2002), "Distributing intelligence and organizing diversity in new-media projects," *Environment and Planning A*, **34**(11), 1927–49.

Girard, M. & D. Stark (2003), "Heterarchies of values in Manhattan-based new media firms," *Theory, Culture, & Society*, **20**(3), 77–105.

Gordon, K. & M. Miyake (2000), "Business approaches to combating bribery: a study of codes of conduct," *OECD Working Papers on International Investment*, No. 2000/01.

Grant, W. (ed.) (1987), *Business Interests: Organisational Development and Private Interest Government*, Berlin: de Gruyter.

Grove, A. (1996), *Only Paranoids Survive*, New York: Doubleday.

Gulati, R., P. Puranam & M. Tushman (2012), "Meta-organization design: rethinking design in interorganizational and community contexts," *Strategic Management Journal*, **33**(6), 571–86.

Gunderson, L. & C.S. Holling (2001), *Panarchy: Understanding Transformations in Systems of Humans and Nature*, Washington, DC: Island Press.

Gupta, A.K. & L.J. Lad (1983), "Industry self-regulation: an economic, organizational, and political analysis," *Academy of Management Review*, **8**(3), 416–25.

Halliday, T.C., M.J. Powell & M.W. Granfors (1987), "Minimalist organizations: vital events in state bar associations, 1870–1930," *American Sociological Review*, **52**(4), 456–71.

Hamilton, A. (1787), "The union as a safeguard against domestic faction and insurrection," *Federalist Papers*, No. 9, for *The Independent Journal*, accessed 15 March 2020 at https://www.congress.gov/resources/display/content/The+Federalist+Papers#TheFederalistPapers-9.

Hansen, J.M. (1985), "The political economy of group membership," *American Political Science Review*, **79**(1), 79–96.

Heckelman, J.C. (2007), "Explaining the rain: the rise and decline of nations after 25 years," *Southern Economic Journal*, **74**(1), 18–33.

Heckman, L. (2011), *How to Find Business Information*, Santa Barbara, CA and Oxford, UK: Praeger.

Hilbert, F.W. (1912), "Employers' associations in the United States," in J.H. Hollander & G.E. Barnett (eds), *Studies in American Trade Unionism*, New York: Henry Holt & Co., pp. 183–217.

Hillman, A.J. & M.A. Hitt (1999), "Corporate political strategy formulation: a model of approach, participation and strategy decisions," *Academy of Management Review*, **24**(4), 825–42.

Hirschman, A.O. (1970), *Exit, Voice and Loyalty: Response to Decline in Firms, Organizations and States*, Cambridge, MA: Harvard University Press.

Jessop, B. (1998), "The rise of governance and the risks of failure: the case of economic development," *International Social Science Journal*, **50**(155), 29–45.

Jimenez, G. (1996), "The International Chamber of Commerce: suppliers of standards and instruments for international trade," *Uniform Law Review*, **1**(2), 284–99.

Kahl, S.J. (2018), "The role of trade associations in market discourse and cognition," *Journal of Management Inquiry*, **27**(1), 13–15.

Kaplan, E. (1972), *Japan: The Government–Business Relationship*, Washington, DC: Department of Commerce.

Kell, G. (2005), "The global compact: selected experiences and reflections," *Journal of Business Ethics*, **59**(1–2), 69–79.

King, A.A., M.J. Lenox & M.L. Barnett (2002), "Strategic responses to the reputation commons problem," in A. Hoffman & M.J. Ventresca (eds), *Organizations, Policy and the Natural Environment: Institutional and Strategic Perspectives*, Stanford, CA: Stanford University Press, pp. 393–406.

Kogut, B. & C. Ragin (2006), "Exploring complexity when diversity is limited: institutional complementarity in theories of rule of law and national systems revisited," *European Management Review*, **3**(1), 44–59.

König, A., M. Schulte & A. Enders (2012), "Inertia in response to non-paradigmatic change: the case of meta-organizations," *Research Policy*, **41**(8), 1325–43.

Kontopoulos, K. (1993), *The Logics of Social Structure*, New York: Cambridge University Press.

Lacombrade, P. (2002), "La chambre de commerce, Paris et le capitalisme français *(1890–1914)*" [The chamber of commerce, Paris and French capitalism (1890–1914)], doctoral thesis, Paris Nanterre University, France.

Lampel, J. & A.D. Meyer (2008), "Field-configuring events as structuring mechanisms: how conferences, ceremonies, and trade shows constitute new technologies, industries, and markets," *Journal of Management Studies*, **45**(6), 1025–35.

Lanzalaco, L. (1992), "Coping with heterogeneity: peak associations of business within and across Western European nations," in J. Greenwood, J. Grote & K. Ronit (eds), *Organized Interests and the European Community*, Newbury Park, CA: Sage, pp. 173–205.

Laumann, E. & D. Knoke (1987), *The Organizational State: Social Choice in National Policy Domains*, Madison, WI: University of Wisconsin Press.

Laumann, E. & D. Knoke (1988), "The increasingly organizational state," *Society*, **25**(2), 21–8.

Lawton, T.S. & T.S. Rajwani (eds) (2015), *The Routledge Companion to Non-Market Strategy*, Abingdon, UK and New York: Routledge.

Lawton, T.C., T.S. Rajwani & A. Minto (2018), "Why trade associations matter: exploring function, meaning, and influence," *Journal of Management Inquiry*, **27**(1), 5–9.

Lenox, M. & J. Nash (2003), "Industry self-regulation and adverse selection: a comparison across four trade association programs," *Business Strategy and the Environment*, **12**(6), 343–56.

Levy, D.L. (2008), "Political contestation in global production networks," *The Academy of Management Review*, **33**(4), 943–63.

Lippmann, S. & H.E. Aldrich (2016), "A rolling stone gathers momentum: generational units, collective memory, and entrepreneurship," *Academy of Management Review*, **41**(4), 658–5.

Liu, K.-C. (1988), "Chinese merchant guilds: an historical inquiry," *Pacific Historical Review*, **57**(1), 1–23.

Lobo, S. (2014), "Auf dem Weg in die Dumpingholle" [On the way to dumping hell], *Der Spiegel*, 3 September 2014, accessed 19 March 2020 at https://www.spiegel.de/netzwelt/netzpolitik/sascha-lobo-sharing-economy-wie-bei-uber-ist-plattform-kapitalismus-a-989584.html.

Locke, R.M. & K. Thelen (1995), "Apples and oranges revisited: contextualized comparisons and the study of comparative labor politics," *Politics and Society*, **23**(3), 337–67.

Luhmann, N. (1992), *Social Systems*, Stanford, CA: Stanford University Press.

Lynn, L.H. & T.J. McKeown (1988), *Organizing Business: Trade Associations in America and Japan*, Washington, DC: American Enterprise Institute for Policy Research.

Madison, J. (1787), "The same subject continued: the union as a safeguard against domestic faction and insurrection," *Federalist Papers*, No. 10, accessed 15 March 2020 at https://www.congress.gov/resources/display/content/The+Federalist+Papers#TheFederalistPapers-10.

Magnusson, L. (1994), "Les institutions d'une économie de marché: le cas de la Suède" [Market economy institutions: the case of Sweden], *Revue du Nord*, **76**(307), 839–52.

March, J. (1962), "The business firm as a political coalition," *The Journal of Politics*, **24**(2), 662–78.

Marques, J.C. (2017), "Industry business associations: self-interested or socially conscious?" *Journal of Business Ethics*, **143**(4), 733–51.

Mayntz, R. (1993), "Modernization and the logic of interorganizational networks," in J. Child, M. Crozier & R. Mayntz et al. (eds), *Societal Change Between Market and Organization*, Aldershot: Avebury, pp. 3–18.

McCormick, L.E. (1996), "A life-cycle model of manufacturing networks and Chicago's metalworking industry," PhD dissertation, Department of Urban Studies and Planning, MIT, USA.

McFarland, A.S. (1991), "Interest groups and political time: cycles in America," *British Journal of Political Science*, **21**(3), 257–84.

McIvor, A.J. (1996), *Organised Capital: Employers' Associations and Industrial Relations in Northern England (1880-1939)*, Cambridge, UK: Cambridge University Press.

McRobie, G. et al. (1957), *Industrial Trade Associations. Activities and Organization*, London: George Allen & Unwin Ltd.

Mele, V. & D.H. Schepers (2013), "E pluribus unum? Legitimacy issues and multi-stakeholder codes of conduct," *Journal of Business Ethics*, **118**(3), 561–76.

Merry, S.E. (2011), "Measuring the world: indicators, human rights, and global governance," *Current Anthropology*, **52**(S3), 583–95.

Michels, R. (1915), *Political Parties: A Sociological Study of the Oligarchical Tendencies of Modern Democracy*, New York: The Free Press.

Miner, A.S., T.L. Amburgey & T.M. Stearns (1990) "Interorganizational linkages and population dynamics: buffering and transformational shields," *Administrative Science Quarterly*, **35**(4), 689–713.

Nank, R. & J. Alexander (2012) "Farewell to Tocqueville's dream: a case study of trade associations and advocacy," *Public Administration Quarterly*, **36**(4), 429–61.

Nash, J. (2002), "The emergence of trade associations as agents of environmental performance improvement," research paper, Sociotechnical Systems Research Center, MIT, accessed 10 March 2020 at https://dspace.mit.edu/handle/1721.1/1604.

Naylor, E.H. (1917), *The Value of Trade Associations*, New York: Alexander Hamilton Institute.

Naylor, E.H. (1921), *Trade Associations: Their Organization and Management*, New York: The Ronald Press Company.

Nicholls, A. & B. Huybrechts (2016), "Sustaining inter-organizational relationships across institutional logics and power asymmetries: the case of fair trade," *Journal of Business Ethics*, **135**(4), 699–714.

Nownes, A.J. (2006), *Total Lobbying: What Lobbyists Want (and How They Try to Get It)*, New York: Cambridge University Press.

Oberman, W.D. (2008), "A conceptual look at the strategic resource dynamics of public affairs," *Journal of Public Affairs*, **8**(4), 249–60.

O'Keefe, P. (2019), "11: FTD – Say it with flowers," *Creative Review*, accessed 17 March 2020 at https://www.creativereview.co.uk/say-it-with-flowers/.

Olson, M. (1965), *The Logic of Collective Action*, Cambridge, MA: Harvard University Press.

Olson, M. (1982), *The Rise and Decline of Nations: Economic Growth, Stagflation and Social Rigidities*, New Haven, CT: Yale University Press.

Parker Follett, M. (2013), *Dynamic Administration: The Collected Papers of Mary Parker Follett*, edited by Henry C. Metcalf & L. Urwick, Mansfield Centre, CT: Martino Publishing.

Pearce, C. (1941), *Monograph No. 18: Trade Association Survey. Investigation of Concentration of Economic Power. A Study Made under the Auspices of the Department of Commerce for the United States Senate, Temporary National Economic Committee, Seventy-Sixth Congress, Third Session*, Washington, DC: Government Printing Office.

Pettigrew, A.M. (1990), "Longitudinal field research on change: theory and practice," *Organization Science*, **1**(3), 267–92.

Piore, M. (2006), "Qualitative research: does it fit economics?" *European Management Review*, **3**(1), 17–23.

Pollack, M.A. (1997), "Delegation, agency, and agenda setting in the European Community," *International Organization*, **51**(1), 99–134.

Potoski, M. & A. Prakash (2005), "Green clubs and voluntary governance: ISO 14001 and firms' regulatory compliance," *American Journal of Political Science*, **49**(2), 235–48.

Powell, W.W. (1990), "Neither market nor hierarchy: network forms of organization," in B. Staw & L.L. Cummings (eds), *Research in Organizational Behavior (Volume 12)*, Greenwich, CT: JAI Press, pp. 295–336.

Prakash, A. & M. Potoski (2007), "Collective action through voluntary environmental programs: a club theory perspective," *The Policy Studies Journal*, **35**(4), 773–92.

Ragin, C. (1987), *The Comparative Method: Moving Beyond Qualitative and Quantitative Strategies*, Berkeley, CA: University of California Press.

Ragin, C. (2000), *Fuzzy-Set Social Science*, Chicago, IL: University of Chicago Press.

Rajwani, T., T. Lawton & N. Phillips (2015), "The 'voice of industry': why management researchers should pay more attention to trade associations," *Strategic Organization*, **13**(3), 224–32.

Rasche, A. & D.U. Gilbert (2012), "Institutionalizing global governance: the role of the United Nations Global Compact," *Business Ethics: A European Review*, **21**(1), 100–114.

Raymond, M. & L. DeNardis (2015), "Multistakeholderism: anatomy of an inchoate global institution," *International Theory*, **7**(3), 572–616.

Reihlen, M. & M. Mone (2012), "Professional service firms, knowledge-based competition, and the heterarchical organization form," in M. Reihlen & A. Werr (eds), *Handbook of Research on Entrepreneurship in Professional Services*, Cheltenham, UK and Northampton, MA, USA: Edward Elgar Publishing, pp. 107–26.

Reinicke, W.H. (1999–2000), "The other World Wide Web: global public policy networks," *Foreign Policy*, No. 117, 44–57.

Reveley, J. & S. Ville (2010), "Enhancing industry association theory: a comparative business history contribution," *Journal of Management Studies*, **47**(5), 837–58.

Roloff, J. (2008), "Learning from multi-stakeholder networks: issue-focussed stakeholder management," *Journal of Business Ethics*, **82**(1), 233–50.

Ronfeldt, D. (1996), "Tribes, institutions, markets, networks: a framework about societal evolution," research paper, RAND Corporation, accessed 17 March 2020 at https://www.rand.org/pubs/papers/P7967.html.

Rosch, E. (1978), "Principles of categorization," in E. Rosch & B.B. Lloyd (eds), *Cognition and Categorization*, Hillsdale: NJ: Lawrence Erlbaum, pp. 27–48.

Rosch, E. & C.B. Mervis (1975), "Family resemblances: studies in the internal structure of categories," *Cognitive Psychology*, **7**(4), 573–605.

Rousseau J.-J. (1762 [2019]), *On the Social Contract* (2nd edition), translated by Donald A. Cress, Cambridge, MA: Hackett Publishing Company.

Ruggie, J.G. (2002), "The theory and practice of learning networks corporate social responsibility and the global compact," *Journal of Corporate Citizenship*, No. 5, 27–36.

Schmitter, P.C. & W. Streeck (1999), "The organization of business interests: studying the associative action of business in advanced industrial societies," *MPIfG Discussion Paper*, No. 99/1.

Schneiberg, M. & R. Hollingsworth (1991), "Can transaction cost economics explain trade associations?" in R.M. Czada & A. Windhoff-Héritier (eds), *Political Choice: Institutions, Rules and the Limits of Rationality*, Boulder, CO: Westview Press, pp 199–256.

Scholz, T. (2017), "Platform cooperativism vs. the sharing economy," in N. Douais & S. Wan (eds), *Big Data and Civil Engagement*, Rome: Planum, pp. 47–51.

Schuler, D.A. (2002), "Public affairs, issues management and political strategy: methodological approaches that count," *Journal of Political Affairs*, **1**(4), 336–55.

Seawright, J. & J. Gerring (2008), "Case selection techniques in case study research: a menu of qualitative and quantitative options," *Political Research Quarterly*, **61**(2), 294–308.

Seidl, D. & F. Werle (2018), "Inter-organizational sensemaking in the face of strategic meta-problems: requisite variety and dynamics of participation," *Strategic Management Journal*, **39**(3), 830–58.

Selsky, J.W. & B. Parker (2005), "Cross-sector partnerships to address social issues: challenges to theory and practice," *Journal of Management*, **31**(6), 849–73.

Sethi, S.P. & D.H. Schepers (2014), "United Nations Global Compact: the promise–performance gap," *Journal of Business Ethics*, **122**(2), 193–208.

Sklar, M.J. (1990), "Sherman Antitrust Act jurisprudence and federal policy-making in the formative period, 1890–1914," *New York Law School Law Review*, **35**(4), 791–826.

Soubiran-Paillet, F. (1993), "Aux origines de la peur des groupements professionnels au XIXᵉ siècle: la législation de la Constituante" [The origins of fear of professional groups in the nineteenth century: the legislation of the Constituent], *Revue Historique*, **289**(1), 149–68.

Spillman, L. (2012), *Solidarity in Strategy: Making Business Meaningful in American Trade Associations*, Chicago, IL: University of Chicago Press.

Spillman, L. (2018), "Meta-organization matters," *Journal of Management Inquiry*, **27**(1), 16–20.

Staber, U. (1987), "Structural constraints on associative action in business: an empirical investigation," *Canadian Journal of Administrative Sciences/Revue Canadienne des Sciences de l'Administration*, **4**(3), 252–65.

Staber, U. & H. Aldrich (1983), "Trade association stability and public policy," in R.H. Hall & R.E. Quinn (eds), *Organization Theory and Public Policy*, Beverly Hills, CA: SAGE, pp. 163–78.

Stark, D. (2009), *The Sense of Dissonance: Accounts of Worth in Economic Life*, Princeton, NJ: Princeton University Press.

Strange, S. (1996), *The Retreat of the State: The Diffusion of Power in the World Economy*, Cambridge, UK: Cambridge University Press.

Streeck, W., J.R. Grote, V. Schneider & J. Visser (eds) (2006), *Governing Interests: Business Associations Facing Internationalism*, Abingdon, UK and New York: Routledge.

Streeck, W. & P.C. Schmitter (eds) (1985a), *Private Interest Government: Beyond Market and State*, London: SAGE.

Streeck, W. & P.C. Schmitter (1985b), "Community, market, state – and associations? The prospective contribution of interest governance to social order," *European Sociological Review*, **1**(2), 119–38.

Taylor, M. & S. Singleton (1993), "The communal resource: transaction costs and the solution of collective action problems," *Politics & Society*, **21**(2), 195–214.

Tilton, M. (1996), *Restrained Trade: Cartels in Japan's Basic Materials Industries*, Ithaca, NY: Cornell University Press.

Tucker, A. (2008), "Trade associations as industry reputation agents: a model of reputational trust," *Business and Politics*, **10**(1), 1–26.

United Nations Global Compact (UNGC) (2008), *The Practical Guide to the United Nations Global Compact Communication on Progress (COP)*, New York: United Nations, accessed 19 March 2020 at http://www.undp.org/content/dam/turkey/docs/Publications/PovRed/Practical_Guide_2008_En.pdf.

U.S. Department of Commerce (1927), *Trade Associations Activities*, Washington, DC: U.S. Government Printing Office.

U.S. Supreme Court (2014), *Eastern States Lumber Ass'n v. United States*, 234 U.S. 600 (2014), accessed 22 March 2020 at https://supreme.justia.com/cases/federal/us/234/600/.

Utting, P. (2002), "Regulating business via multistakeholder initiatives: a preliminary assessment," United Nations Research Institute for Social Development research paper.

Van Parijs, P. (2002), "The spotlight and the microphone: must business be socially responsible, and can it?" *Chair Hoover Working* Paper, No. 92, Catholic University of Louvain, Belgium.

Vogel, D. (2005), *The Market for Virtue: The Potential and Limits of Corporate Social Responsibility*, Washington, DC: Brookings Institution Press.

von Schnurbein, G. (2009), "Patterns of governance structures in trade associations and unions," *Nonprofit Management and Leadership*, **20**(1), 97–115.

Wallerstein, M. (1984), "Review of *The Rise and Decline of Nations*," *Ethics*, **94**(2), 348–50.

Waters, M. (1989), "Collegiality, bureaucratization, and professionalization: a Weberian analysis," *American Journal of Sociology*, **94**(5), 945–72.

Westerman, P. (2018), *Outsourcing the Law: A Philosophical Perspective on Regulation*, Cheltenham, UK and Northampton, MA, USA: Edward Elgar Publishing.

Williams, O.F. (2004), "The UN Global Compact: the challenge and the promise," *Business Ethics Quarterly*, **14**(4), 755–74.

Willoughby, W.F. (1905), "Employers' associations for dealing with labor in the United States," *Quarterly Journal of Economics*, **20**, 110–50.

Wilson, J.Q. (1973), *Political Organizations*, New York: Basic Books.

Wilson, J.Q. (ed.) (1980), *The Politics of Regulation*, New York: Basic Books.

Winn, M.I., P. MacDonald & C. Zietsma (2008), "Managing industry reputation: the dynamic tension between collective and competitive reputation management strategies," *Corporate Reputation Review*, **11**(1), 35–55.

Wittgenstein (1953 [2008]), *Philosophical Investigations: 50th Anniversary Commemorative Edition*, Oxford: Basil Blackwell.

Yami, S., S. Castaldo, G.B. Dagnino & F. Le Roy (2010), *Coopetition: Winning Strategies for the 21st Century*, Cheltenham, UK and Northampton, MA, USA: Edward Elgar Publishing.

Yarmie, A.H. (1980), "Employers' organizations in mid-Victorian England," *International Review of Social History*, **25**(2), 209–35.

Yin, R.K. (2003), *Case Study Research: Design and Methods* (3rd edition), Thousand Oaks, CA: SAGE.

Index